WORDLY WISE 3000®

3000®
SECOND EDITION

Book **11**

Kenneth Hodkinson | Sandra Adams

EDUCATORS PUBLISHING SERVICE
Cambridge and Toronto

Original cover design: Hugh Price
Interior design: Sarah Cole
Acquisitions/Development: Kate Moltz
Editors: Wendy Drexler, Elissa Gershowitz, Stacey Nichols Kim, Theresa Trinder, Laura Woollett
Editorial Assistant: Becky Ticotsky
Senior Editorial Manager: Sheila Neylon

Printed in the U.S.A.

ISBN 0-8388-2829-9
978-0-8388-2829-8
2 3 4 5 CURW 11 10 09 08 07

Contents

Lesson 1

Word List
Study the definitions of the words below; then do the exercises for the lesson.

apocryphal
ə päk´ re fəl

adj. Of dubious authenticity or origin; spurious.
Although we hear numerous stories of Daniel Boone's exploits, many of them are **apocryphal**.

arcane
är kān´

adj. Understood by only a few; mysterious.
To most people, the science of quantum physics is an **arcane** subject that is beyond their grasp.

convene
kən vēn´

v. 1. To summon or cause to assemble.
The president has **convened** a meeting of his economic advisors for this Thursday.
2. To gather or assemble; to meet formally.
Student Council members **convene** on the first Monday of the month.

expedient
ek spē´ dē ənt

adj. 1. Useful for some purpose; convenient.
Telephoning was the most **expedient** method of alerting Sara to our change of plan.
2. Concerned primarily or exclusively with serving one's own interests.
Given a choice, Ray does what is **expedient** rather than what is right.
n. A means employed to bring about a certain result.
A hot bath is a useful **expedient** for ameliorating sore muscles.

exude
eg zo͞od´

v. 1. To flow out slowly; to ooze or emit.
The pine branch **exuded** golden pitch after it was cut.
2. To give forth; to exhibit in abundance.
A good lawyer **exudes** confidence no matter how her case is going.

gesticulate
jes tik´ yo͞o lāt

v. To motion energetically with the body or limbs.
The traffic cop **gesticulated** to the waiting cars to proceed.
gesticulation *n.*
We were puzzled by Will's frantic **gesticulations** until we noticed the bee buzzing around his head.

imperturbable
im pər tʉr´ bə bəl

adj. Calm and assured.
Picking up the phone to call the plumber, my mother remained **imperturbable**.

increment
in´ krə mənt

n. An increase, addition or gain, often by regular, consecutive amounts.
Even small increments to a savings account add up to a substantial sum over time.
incremental *adj.* (in krə ment´l)
Incremental changes to the dosage of Sunil's medication were necessary to maintain its effectiveness.

levity
lev´ ə tē

n. Excessive frivolity; a lack of seriousness; joking.
The atmosphere at the party was one of **levity** with much joking, laughter, and general silliness.

mortify
môr´ tə fī

v. To embarrass or humiliate.
Jason's fall to the ice just as he was ready to fire the puck past the goalie **mortified** him for days.

periphery pə rif´ ər ē	*n.* The area around the edges; the outermost part. Hesitant to enter the walled garden, Joy made her way instead along the **periphery**. **peripheral** *adj.* Relating to, involving, or forming an outer edge or boundary. Bill Bradley's extraordinary **peripheral** vision allowed him to see more of the basketball court than his opponents.
raconteur ra kän tər´	(A French word now part of our vocabulary.) *n.* One who tells stories with skill and wit. Aunt Clara knew so many stories and was such a superb **raconteur** that she could entertain us for hours.
reiterate rē it´ ər āt	*v.* To say or do over again; to repeat. The signs posted at fifty-foot intervals **reiterate** the warning against hunting.
subterfuge sub´ tər fyoōj	*n.* A deceptive scheme or strategy. Friar Laurence's **subterfuge** to bring Romeo and Juliet together not only deceived their families, but also came to a terrible end.
vacillate vas´ ə lāt	*v.* 1. To move back and forth from lack of balance; waver. The needle **vacillated** between 5 and 6 before registering 5.4 on the Richter scale. 2. To alternate indecisively between opinions or courses of action. Karen's summer plans are still not set because she is **vacillating** between a cross-country bike ride and an internship with the science museum.

1A Understanding Meanings

Read the sentences below. If a sentence correctly uses the word in bold, write *C* on the line below it. If a sentence is incorrect, rewrite it so that the vocabulary word in bold is used correctly.

1. Persons who **convene** come together in a group.

_____

apocryphal

arcane

convene

expedient

exude

gesticulate

imperturbable

increment

levity

mortify

periphery

raconteur

reiterate

subterfuge

vacillate

2. An **imperturbable** person is one who gets upset easily.

_____

3. **Peripheral** matters are those that are not central.

_____

4. To **reiterate** a concern is to express it over and over again.

_____

5. A **subterfuge** is a comment that is not intended to be heard.

_____

6. To **exude** confidence is to exhibit it in abundance.

7. **Incremental** changes are those made gradually.

8. A **raconteur** is a person who is skilled at deceiving others.

9. To **gesticulate** is to say or express something by making gestures.

10. An **expedient** is a means to accomplishing an end.

11. To **mortify** someone is to cause that person's death.

12. **Levity** is a state of perfect balance.

13. An **arcane** theory is one that not many people understand.

14. To **vacillate** is to keep changing one's mind.

15. An **apocryphal** event is one of earth-shaking significance.

1B Using Words

If the word (or a form of the word) in bold fits in a sentence in the group below it, write the word in the blank. If the word does not fit, leave the space empty.

1. **exude**

   (a) Moisture from the body is _____ through the pores of the skin.

   (b) As soon as Tom _____ the speed limit, he was stopped by the highway patrol.

   (c) The producer _____ such charm that it was hard to refuse his offer.

2. **mortify**

   (a) When I went to pay the check, I was _____ to discover that I had no money.

   (b) The _____ professor realized too late that she had given her students the wrong exam.

   (c) Fortunately, the dog was not _____ when the car struck it.

3. **vacillate**

   (a) Dr. Shin _____ the baby against a variety of diseases.

   (b) Ayesha _____ the drink until all the ingredients were combined.

   (c) My little sister _____ between a party at home and a trip to the ice-skating rink for her birthday.

4. **raconteur**

   (a) Abraham Lincoln was an excellent _____ with a fund of interesting stories.

   (b) Leslie forgot the punch line, so we never found out how the _____ ended.

   (c) A good _____ pays close attention to the response of the listeners.

5. **gesticulate**

   (a) Secretary Braun said she had _____ several ideas in her mind that might help us solve the problem.

   (b) The baby wriggled and laughed when we _____ her tummy.

   (c) He _____ so much when he talked that I paid more attention to his arms than to his story.

6. **apocryphal**

   (a) A nuclear war would be the most _____ event in human history.

   (b) I never know when she's being _____ and when she's telling the truth.

   (c) We dismissed these accounts of UFO contacts with humans as _____ .

7. **expedient**

   (a) Guessing is the unprepared person's _____ for coping with tests.

   (b) In view of the heavy rains, it may be _____ to delay the spring planting.

   (c) Nations sometimes do what is politically _____ without regard to morality.

apocryphal

arcane

convene

expedient

exude

gesticulate

imperturbable

increment

levity

mortify

periphery

raconteur

reiterate

subterfuge

vacillate

8. **convene**

(a) I _____ Robert's message to the members of his family.

(b) The manager _____ so many meetings that little actual work got done.

(c) All the teachers _____ after school to discuss whether to introduce Spanish in grade four.

1C Word Study

Choose from the two words provided and use each word only once when filling in the spaces. Once space should be left blank.

vacillate/waver

1. Juan will _____ for hours over whether to stay or go.

2. Charlotte's determination to take part in the event began to _____ .

3. The boat began to _____ , and seconds later it sank.

exudes/emits

4. A successful speaker _____ confidence on the platform.

5. The newest engine _____ very little carbon dioxide.

6. Ms. Ruiz _____ words of wisdom to whoever will listen.

arcane/mysterious

7. The walls were painted in bright _____ colors to create a cheerful effect.

8. We never found out what caused the _____ noise in the cellar.

9. The high priests possessed _____ knowledge denied to ordinary Romans.

apocryphal/spurious

10. The _____ signature on the document made the lease invalid.

11. Many of Uncle Sayed's stories are _____ , but we enjoy hearing them.

12. Lindsay learned that the diamond in her ring is almost certainly _____ .

expedient/convenient

13. I felt that the most _____ thing was to say nothing at all about the matter.

14. I notice that Susannah has grown increasingly _____ since she took up sports.

15. Using the Internet is a(n) _____ way to shop.

1D Images of Words

Circle the letter of each sentence that suggests the numbered bold vocabulary word. In each group, you may circle more than one letter or none at all.

1. **imperturbable**

   (a) There was not enough breeze to fill the sails, so Carrie started the engine.

   (b) Robin studies, oblivious to her siblings playing loudly around her.

   (c) The little boy stuck out his tongue at me and then turned and ran.

2. **expedient**

   (a) When we heard that a blizzard was forecast, we decided to return home.

   (b) To guarantee that the package arrives tomorrow, you should use the express service.

   (c) The candidate reversed his position on gun control when he saw the latest polls.

3. **levity**

   (a) The new fighter jet soared to 20,000 feet in less than a minute.

   (b) I always enjoy reading the jokes in this magazine.

   (c) The banter and loud laughter emanating from the next table prevented us from enjoying our meal.

4. **reiterate**

   (a) When Pam got off the roller coaster, she wanted to get right back on again.

   (b) The sick child kept saying, "I want my mommy."

   (c) The phone rang repeatedly, but no one bothered to answer it.

5. **apocryphal**

   (a) George Washington, as a boy, did not chop down his father's cherry tree.

   (b) For three days in a row, the local weather forecast was wrong.

   (c) Mark Twain said that reports of his death had been "greatly exaggerated."

6. **incremental**

   (a) Last night's six inches of snow brings the month's total to 58 inches.

   (b) Men's jacket sizes are 36-inch, 38-inch, 40-inch, 42-inch, and 44-inch.

   (c) Her starting salary was $34,000, but each year she received a $1,000 raise until she was earning $40,000 a year.

7. **vacillate**

   (a) The baby cried when the nurse gave her a measles shot.

   (b) Color variations make the bark of the sycamore tree distinctive.

   (c) The car skidded on the ice and went off the road into the guard rail.

apocryphal
arcane
convene
expedient
exude
gesticulate
imperturbable
increment
levity
mortify
periphery
raconteur
reiterate
subterfuge
vacillate

8. **arcane**

   (a) Karl Marx's theory of labor is understood by very few people.

   (b) Gary has trouble understanding simple addition and subtraction.

   (c) Few people outside of south-central Chile can speak Araucan.

9. **peripheral**

   (a) Since she worked only one day a week, Ms. Dawson had little to do with the project.

   (b) Pluto, the most distant planet in our solar system, is billions of miles from the sun.

   (c) The story that Davy Crockett killed a bear when he was only three is false.

10. **subterfuge**

    (a) The fountain is supplied with water from an underground pipe.

    (b) The Greeks are said to have penetrated Troy's defenses by hiding inside a wooden horse.

    (c) The man entered the house by posing as an inspector for the gas company.

1E Passage

Read the passage below; then complete the exercise that follows it.

Going, Going, Gone!

A man attending an auction absent-mindedly scratches his ear and, within a few minutes, is **mortified** to learn that with this casual movement he has bought a stuffed and mounted moose head complete with antlers. The story, though **apocryphal**, is a staple of auction folklore and expresses the fear that some people have of being drawn unwittingly into the bidding fray. The fear is unjustified. Bidding in public auctions is usually done by **gesticulating** in the auctioneer's direction while holding a numbered card aloft. The possibility of anyone making an unintended offer under these circumstances is slight.

In the **arcane** world of private, fine art auction houses, events are conducted with conspicuous restraint. Most people attending such auctions are known to the auctioneer and to each other because many are dealers who come to buy for their own business or for private clients. As the **imperturbable** auctioneer presides over the sale of an item whose price may eventually reach tens of millions of dollars, a person may bid by doing nothing more than catching the auctioneer's eye. In contrast, tugging an ear or looking up at the ceiling may be signals arranged beforehand with the auctioneer to indicate a desire to withdraw from the bidding.

The success of any auction, whether public or private, depends to a great degree on the skill of the person conducting the auction. A good auctioneer must be something of a **raconteur**, with a fund of amusing stories to tell and the wit to keep them brief. Often, by using a little **levity**, he or she can relax the crowd and help the bids flow more freely.

Various **subterfuges** are commonly employed to create interest and maintain alertness in the audience. The auctioneer may cry "Sold!" just as the bidding is getting underway. One lucky person gets a valuable item for a song, and the rest learn that if they **vacillate**, a bargain may slip away. Auctioneers have even been known to drop a (not very valuable) vase as an **expedient** to get the attention of a crowd that seems to be drifting into boredom.

Given the large number of auctions held in the United States each year, there is an increasing demand for people qualified to conduct them. This demand is met in large part by schools for auctioneers. The oldest and largest of these is the Missouri Auction School in Kansas City, founded in 1905. It **convenes** four times a year for intensive nine-day courses. These are attended by up to one thousand men and women of all ages and walks of life hoping to become professional auctioneers.

Doing their best to **exude** the kind of confidence auctioneers must demonstrate, students conduct mock auctions with the rest of the class acting as potential bidders. They learn to develop their **peripheral** vision so as not to miss bids from the side of the hall, and they get a chance to practice the uniquely American style of conducting auctions in a singsong chant. An uninterrupted flow of words is punctuated by **reiterated** reminders of the last bid, followed by the bid the auctioneer would like to get from the audience. His or her chant might go like this: ". . . . *thirty* dollar bid an' now forty, now forty . . . *thirty* dollar bid and *willya* gimme forty . . . *thirty* dollar bid an' now five . . . *thirty-five* dollar bid and *willya* gimme forty . . . "

Why the chant? One practical reason is that it places less strain on the auctioneer's voice than saying the same words for long periods of time. In addition, the rhythmical pattern of speech often helps draw and maintain the attention of the audience. Finally, as one student of auctions has explained, "Chanting makes less obvious the sometimes long, quiet intervals between bids, thus obscuring the fact that the bidding is anything but lively."

Auctions are a popular form of entertainment in the United States. Whether the bidding increases in **increments** of five dollars or, as in important art auctions, in hundreds of thousands of dollars, they offer excitement, suspense, and, occasionally, high drama. Perhaps this explains why millions of Americans attend auctions each year.

Answer each of the following questions in the form of a sentence. If a question does not contain a vocabulary word from this lesson's word list, use one in your answer. Use each word only once.

1. Why might a very good **raconteur** make a poor auctioneer?

2. What possibilities for training exist for people who want to become auctioneers?

3. When do you think it would be most important for an auctioneer to be **imperturbable**?

4. How does the passage make clear that the moose head story may be untrue?

5. What is one skill both ball players and auctioneers need to cultivate?

6. How might a good auctioneer add **levity** to an auction?

apocryphal

arcane

convene

expedient

exude

gesticulate

imperturbable

increment

levity

mortify

periphery

raconteur

reiterate

subterfuge

vacillate

7. How do auctioneers make sure their audiences know the last bid that was taken?

8. According to the passage, what is one way the bidding in a private art auction differs from that in a public auction?

9. Describe what you would consider a **mortifying** experience for a bidder.

10. What do auctioneers often use to keep their audience's attention?

11. Why do you think the world of the fine art auction houses is described as **arcane**?

12. What are some **expedients** bidders in fine art auctions use to withdraw from the bidding?

FUN & FASCINATING FACTS

When the King James version of the Bible was published in 1611, the scholars preparing it worked from a Greek translation of the Old Testament made in the third century B.C. Fourteen books were excluded because they were not considered part of the original Jewish scriptures and were of doubtful authenticity. They are called the Apocrypha, from the Greek *apokruphos*, "hidden." The adjective **apocryphal** may refer to these fourteen books or mean "of doubtful authenticity."

Levity is lightness of manner or speech; the word derives from the Latin *levis*, "light in weight." Several other words share this root. To *levitate* is to become so light that one rises up in defiance of gravity. To *alleviate* a person's woes is to lighten them. *Leavened* bread rises through the action of yeast.

Iterate means "to say again." The prefix *re-* means "again;" putting it before *iterate* to form **reiterate** seems repetitious. Actually, the two words are synonyms, but *reiterate*, perhaps because the prefix strengthens the meaning, is more commonly used; *iterate* has become obsolete.

Lesson 2

Word List

Study the definitions of the words below; then do the exercises for the lesson.

accoutrements
ə kōō´ trə mənts

n. pl. Equipment or accessories.
Deborah had two bags for film, lenses, and her other photography **accoutrements**.

aggrieved
ə grēvd´

adj. Feeling or expressing a sense of injustice, injury, or offense.
Hank's **aggrieved** attitude is understandable since he was treated so unfairly.

choleric
käl´ ər ik

adj. Easily angered; quick-tempered.
The coach grew increasingly **choleric** as it became apparent that the players were disobeying his orders.

comport
kəm pôrt´

v. 1. To behave or conduct oneself.
In public Alec was usually solemn, but he **comported** himself quite differently in private.
2. To be in accord or agreement. Used with *with*.
What Naomi stated as policy does not **comport** with what I read in the personnel manual.

disconcert
dis kən surt´

v. To disrupt the self-possession or confidence of; to perturb or fluster.
I was **disconcerted** by my brother's display of levity at the memorial service.
disconcerting *adj.*
Marie found it **disconcerting** to have Sam ask her a question and then to see him ignore her as she began to answer.

fauna
fô´ nə

n. Animals of a region or period, considered as a whole.
The **fauna** of the North American woodlands includes deer, fox, and bear.

interpose
in tər pōz´

v. To place or come between; to intervene or interrupt.
Roberta **interposed** herself between the two children to distract them from their argument.

maraud
mə rôd´

v. To roam in search of plunder.
Centuries ago highwaymen **marauded** the Dover Road, stopping stagecoaches and robbing the passengers.
marauder *n.*
The Vikings were the most infamous **marauders** of all who plundered the North Sea coasts.

modicum
mäd´ ə kəm

n. A small amount.
Republicans thought the tax bill would pass even if it received only a **modicum** of support from the Democrats.

opulent
äp´ yə lənt

adj. Having or exhibiting great wealth or abundance.
Why, she wondered as she leafed through magazines at the newsstand, were there so many articles featuring the **opulent** homes of very rich people?
opulence *n.*
The architecture and furnishings of the palace at Versailles are remarkable for their **opulence**.

patrician pə trish´ ən	*n.* A member of the nobility. Lord Gorton was a **patrician** who found it expedient to pose as a man of the people. *adj.* Of noble birth; showing refinement of taste or manners. Corinne's interests in fine wine and antiques reveal a **patrician** sensibility.
phlegmatic fleg mat´ ik	*adj.* Not given to action or reaction; sluggish or calm in temperament. Although Breon was a **phlegmatic** child, she grew into an active, decisive teenager.
propensity prə pen´ sə tē	*n.* A natural inclination or tendency. My mother has a **propensity** for bursting into song when something in a conversation reminds her of a particular verse.
therapeutic ther ə pyōō´ tik	*adj.* Relating to the treatment of a disease; contributing to general well-being. A doctor who exudes kindness can have a **therapeutic** effect on the patient.
utilitarian yōō til ə ter´ ē ən	*adj.* Relating to usefulness rather than beauty; practical. The phrase "form follows function" reflects a **utilitarian** approach to design.

2A Understanding Meanings

Read the sentences below. If a sentence correctly uses the word in bold, write *C* on the line below it. If a sentence is incorrect, rewrite it so that the vocabulary word in bold is used correctly.

1. To **comport** with the known facts is to represent them falsely.

_____

2. To **maraud** is to roam in search of plunder.

_____

3. An area's **fauna** consists of the animals that are native to it.

_____

4. An **opulent** display is one characterized by rich abundance.

_____

5. **Utilitarian** accommodations are those that provide the bare necessities.

_____

6. A **choleric** person is one who remains imperturbable despite provocation.

_____

7. A **patrician** is a person of noble birth.

8. To **interpose** something is to place it between two things.

9. **Accoutrement**s are little sandwiches served as appetizers.

10. To **disconcert** someone is to exclude that person from consideration.

11. A **modicum** is an essential part of any computer.

12. A **therapeutic** product is one that has healing properties.

13. A **propensity** for hard work is a natural inclination for it.

14. An **aggrieved** person is one who has done an injustice to another.

15. A **phlegmatic** person is one who is imperturbable.

accoutrements
aggrieved
choleric
comport
disconcert
fauna
interpose
maraud
modicum
opulent
patrician
phlegmatic
propensity
therapeutic
utilitarian

2B Using Words

If the word (or a form of the word) in bold fits in a sentence in the group below it, write the word in the blank. If the word does not fit, leave the space empty.

1. **interpose**

   (a) The artist _____ blue and orange to create visual movement in this painting.

   (b) My opponent _____ her pawn between my bishop and her king.

   (c) I hope I did not _____ on you by staying one more night.

2. **modicum**

   (a) The quark of an atomic nucleus is the smallest _____ known to science.

   (b) If he had even a _____ of sensitivity, he would offer you his apologies.

   (c) A _____ of salt is all that is needed to enhance the flavor of the soup.

3. **utilitarian**

   (a) _____ steel desks replaced the ornamental walnut and mahogany ones after the renovation.

   (b) Despite its _____ appearance, the Land Rover is a luxury vehicle.

   (c) Last fall the _____ companies raised their rates on electricity to businesses.

4. **disconcert**

   (a) To find oneself face to face with the president can be _____ .

   (b) The strange look she gave me when I asked her name was quite _____ .

   (c) Are you _____ yourself completely from the project?

5. **comport**

   (a) All of the data gathered so far _____ with the theory of global warming.

   (b) Niels intends to _____ himself as a space alien for Halloween.

   (c) She _____ herself with great dignity despite her difficult circumstances.

6. **aggrieved**

   (a) The _____ party has a right to sue the person who caused the injury.

   (b) I admit that I felt _____ when they left without an explanation or apology.

   (c) The _____ knee should heal in a week if you give it rest.

7. **propensity**

   (a) My father's car has a _____ to pull to the left when I put on the brakes.

   (b) His _____ for having his picture taken as often as possible caused us much amusement.

   (c) Katya was driven by her _____ to graduate early.

8. **patrician**

   (a) You can become a _____ of the theater by donating five hundred dollars.

   (b) Only a _____ could hold high office in the ancient Roman republic.

   (c) Angela could not satisfy her _____ tastes because her work as a daycare teacher paid very poorly.

2C Word Study

Each group of four words below contains two words that are either synonyms or antonyms. Circle these two words, then circle the *S* if they are synonyms, the *A* if they are antonyms.

1. subterfuge	center	opulent	periphery	S	A
2. propensity	modicum	tendency	admission	S	A
3. reduction	fluctuation	levity	increment	S	A
4. utilitarian	detrimental	therapeutic	arcane	S	A
5. accessories	subterfuges	increments	accoutrements	S	A
6. benevolent	apocryphal	phlegmatic	choleric	S	A
7. vacillate	mortify	waver	interpose	S	A
8. reiterate	summon	convene	aggrieve	S	A
9. imperturbable	incremental	apocryphal	excitable	S	A
10. placated	confused	aggrieved	opulent	S	A

2D Images of Words

Circle the letter of each sentence that suggests the numbered bold vocabulary word. In each group, you may circle more than one letter or none at all.

accoutrements
aggrieved
choleric
comport
disconcert
fauna
interpose
maraud
modicum
opulent
patrician
phlegmatic
propensity
therapeutic
utilitarian

1. **maraud**

   (a) The burglars gained entry to the house by breaking a kitchen window.

   (b) Their ship destroyed, the sailors were unable to leave the tiny island.

   (c) Residents barricaded themselves in their homes when the outlaw gang rode into town.

2. **opulence**

   (a) While in Los Angeles, we took the tour of famous movie stars' homes.

   (b) The enormous blossoms that filled the garden gave off a heady perfume.

   (c) A limousine glided up the long driveway to the mansion.

3. **fauna**

   (a) Cactus plants grow in the wild only in the Americas.

   (b) Kangaroos are native to Australia, Tasmania, and New Guinea.

   (c) Canada has a population of about twenty-five million.

4. modicum

(a) The average age of the class was fourteen years and five months.

(b) Even though he only had a few hours of training, Dan was able to use the new computer.

(c) Mary repaid the money in regular installments spread over two years.

5. choleric

(a) The farmer became red in the face and bellowed at us to get off his land.

(b) A cholera epidemic can take many lives.

(c) People quick to anger may put themselves at risk of a heart attack.

6. accoutrements

(a) Each soldier was issued a backpack, a cartridge belt, and a steel helmet.

(b) She wore a plain black skirt, a white blouse, and low-heeled shoes.

(c) I walked to the pier with my rod and reel, a line, some hooks, and sinkers.

7. propensity

(a) Objects fall to earth because of gravity's attractive force.

(b) Aunt Kate tends to pull her earlobe when she is nervous.

(c) This is the fourth time this week that Jarrett has lost his car keys.

8. disconcert

(a) The pipe had become detached from the joint, causing the leak.

(b) We unplugged all the appliances before closing down the summer cottage.

(c) There were no hard feelings when the rock group broke up after two years.

9. therapeutic

(a) Malaria is caused by the bite of the anopheline mosquito.

(b) Applying ice promptly to the affected area reduces the severity of a burn.

(c) Sometimes a hug is all you need when you're feeling discouraged.

10. phlegmatic

(a) The river moved sluggishly as it meandered across the lowlands.

(b) When Grace discovered the full extent of her losses, she just shrugged.

(c) A hush fell over the audience as the conductor raised his baton.

Read the passage below; then complete the exercise that follows it.

Looking at Llamas

The llama, a member of the camel family, is not listed among the **fauna** of North America. Yet since the early 1900s, when they were introduced here from South America, llamas have made themselves at home to such an extent that there are now an estimated fifteen thousand of these remarkable creatures living in the United States. While the first llamas were imported as exotic pets for the wealthy, llamas soon outgrew this limited role as symbols of **opulence**. Their intelligence, affability, and enjoyment of human company, along with their ability to perform many **utilitarian** tasks, soon placed them in demand.

Today, sheep ranchers use llamas to guard their flocks from coyotes and from **marauding** dogs. Attacks by these animals account for more than three quarters of all sheep losses, at a cost approaching one hundred million dollars a year. When shooting, trapping, and poisoning these predators proved ineffectual, sheep ranchers began using llamas to defend their flocks and found them to be extremely protective of their charges. The llama will **interpose** itself between the flock and a threatening coyote or dog; its aggressive posture usually **disconcerts** the attacker sufficiently that it backs off. If it doesn't, the llama will charge. While this usually drives the predator away, occasionally the llama becomes the victim.

Other enthusiastic supporters of llamas are the United States Forest Service and the National Park Service. Rangers from these agencies take advantage of the fact that llamas are extremely independent animals. With a **modicum** of training, they make excellent pack animals. The rangers use them to transport supplies in areas where wheeled vehicles cannot go. Because of their two-toed padded feet, llamas are far less destructive of fragile trails than horses or mules, which have hard hooves. In addition, their **phlegmatic** nature makes them easy to manage, an important consideration since both agencies use volunteers who need extensive training to cope with horses and mules but who require minimal instruction in handling llamas.

Once shown how to perform a task, llamas will do it provided that it interests them. One of the more unusual occupations in which they are employed makes use of this intelligence. Llamas can be found in increasing numbers on the nation's golf courses, acting as caddies. Loaded down with all the golfing **accoutrements** considered necessary for the game, the llamas plod along between holes, wait patiently at the greens, and are said to have a calming effect on those golfers who may become **choleric** after missing an easy putt. Llamas are extremely fastidious and easily trained, so each hole has a toilet area set aside for their use.

accoutrements
aggrieved
choleric
comport
disconcert
fauna
interpose
maraud
modicum
opulent
patrician
phlegmatic
propensity
therapeutic
utilitarian

Even as these accommodating creatures enter more and more occupations, their traditional role as family pets continues. Llamas establish an instant rapport with their owners and are exceptionally gentle with children. A healthy llama can be bought for less than a thousand dollars, but the **patricians** of the llama world, those used for selective breeding, sell for more than fifteen thousand dollars.

One persistent myth about the llama is that it has an unfortunate **propensity** to spit in people's faces. This does not **comport** with the facts. It is true that if it is frightened, it may respond in this way, or if its forbearance is severely tested, an **aggrieved** llama may show its displeasure by spitting. Owners, however, are quick to point out that this behavior is rare and is usually directed at another llama invading its space. So well-disposed are llamas toward people, in fact, that they are playing an important **therapeutic** role in helping people with severe mental illnesses. In one program in South Carolina, patients are each assigned a llama to serve as companion and pack animal on wilderness treks. Human and llama establish a bond, offering the patient an opportunity to relate to another creature in an unthreatening situation. The practice is effective, the program's director says, because "llamas accept you just the way you are."

Answer each of the following questions in the form of a sentence. If a question does not contain a vocabulary word from this lesson's word list, use one in your answer. Use each word only once.

1. What details in the passage suggest that llamas have a **propensity** for human company?

2. What **accoutrements** would you expect llamas to be carrying when they accompany people on a wilderness trek?

3. What is one example from the passage that illustrates that the llama is not always **phlegmatic**?

4. Why are llamas allowed on golf courses?

5. What might happen if a llama becomes **disconcerted**?

6. When did the llama first appear in North America?

7. Why do rangers prefer to use llamas as pack animals in fragile wilderness areas rather than horses or mules?

8. How was the llama's **patrician** status changed by its role as a working animal?

9. What examples in the passage illustrate the **therapeutic** effect llamas have?

10. Why would it be inaccurate to say that llamas are a symbol of **opulence** today?

FUN & FASCINATING FACTS

Physicians of the ancient world believed, and the belief persisted into medieval times, that the body was governed by four fluids called *humors*, from the Latin word for "fluid." These were *sanguineus* (blood), *cholericus* (yellow bile), *melancholicus* (black bile), and *phlegmaticus* (phlegm). Depending on which humor was dominant, a person could be *sanguine* (cheerful), **choleric** (angry), *melancholy* (sad), or **phlegmatic** (easygoing). An imbalance of these four humors made a person ill-humored; when they were in balance, such a person was in good humor, able to laugh or engage in a little levity.

Fauna is a general term for all the animals of a region or geological period. The word comes from Faunus, a Roman god of nature whose followers were called *fauns* and were pictured as having the body of a man along with the horns, ears, tail, and legs of a goat. The equivalent term for plant life is *flora*, derived from Flora, the Roman goddess of flowers.

Early Rome was ruled by the city fathers, who took the name **patrician** from the Latin *pater*, "father." The common people were called *plebeians*, from the Latin *plebius*, "of the common people." The patricians considered themselves more refined than the plebeians, and to this day **patrician** refers to a person with an aristocratic manner.

Lesson 3

Word List
Study the definitions of the words below; then do the exercises for the lesson.

atrophy
a´ trə fē

v. To waste away or fail to develop.
Paralysis of a person's limbs causes the muscles to **atrophy**.

efficacy
ef´ i kə sē

n. The power to bring about the desired result; effectiveness.
The **efficacy** of aspirin as a pain reliever has been proven beyond a doubt.
efficacious *adj.* (ef i kā´ shəs)
Mediation has proven an **efficacious** way of settling disputes.

emolument
i mäl´ yə mənt

n. Salary or fees for work done; compensation.
The **emoluments** the poet received for her readings provided a modicum of income.

icon
ī´ kän

n. 1. A religious painting, especially one revered by the Eastern Christian churches.
The exhibition of early Russian art included an **icon** of Saint Sergius of Radonezh, painted in the fifteenth century.
2. A symbol or image whose form suggests its meaning.
On a computer screen, a small image of a sheet of paper folded at the corner is the **icon** that represents a document.
3. One who is idolized.
The Beatles became **icons** of pop music in the 1960s.

incipient
in sip´ ē ənt

adj. Beginning to exist or appear; in the first stage.
At the **incipient** stage of my cold, Clara insisted that I use some of her zinc lozenges to prevent it from developing further.

inculcate
in kul´ kāt

v. To impress upon or teach by frequent repetition.
My father **inculcated** in me the value of comporting myself with modesty at all times.

inestimable
in es´ tə mə bəl

adj. Too valuable or great to be measured.
The value of a friend you can really rely on is **inestimable**.

lackluster
lak´ lus tər

adj. Lacking brightness or vitality; without spirit or enthusiasm.
The oboe soloist was not pleased with her **lackluster** performance and promised to practice more so she could do better next time.

martinet
märt'n et´

n. A strict disciplinarian.
Summer camp was not at all relaxing because the director was a **martinet** who did not believe in free time.

prodigious
prə dij´ əs

adj. 1. Extremely large in bulk, quantity, or degree.
The runners ate **prodigious** amounts of pasta at dinner the night before the marathon.
2. Causing amazement or wonder.
At the carnival, we took in everything, including a performance by Mr. Muscles, whose **prodigious** feats of strength were, indeed, amazing.

regimen rej´ ə mən	*n.* A regulated program, especially one designed to improve or maintain health. After injuring his knee, Paul faithfully followed the **regimen** of daily exercises recommended by his physical therapist.
stellar stel´ ər	*adj.* 1. Of or related to a star. The Big Dipper, being made of stars, is known as a **stellar** configuration. 2. Outstanding or brilliant. The audience raved over DiCaprio's **stellar** performance.
stoic stō´ ik	*n.* One seemingly indifferent to pleasure or pain. He comported himself like a **stoic** throughout his long and painful ordeal. *adj.* To observers, Beth's **stoic** demeanor revealed little of either her happiness or her sorrow.
vibrant vī´ brənt	*adj.* 1. Full of life or vigor. The raconteur's **vibrant** personality helped make the performance a lively one. 2. Bright or vivid. Reds and oranges are more **vibrant** than greys or browns. 3. Quivering or vibrating. The **vibrant** strings of the guitar transmit sound through the body of the instrument.
zealous zel´ əs	*adj.* Very enthusiastic; fervent; passionate on behalf of someone or something. The candidate's **zealous** supporters convened in the hotel ballroom to pledge their wholehearted support.

3A Understanding Meanings

Read the sentences below. If a sentence correctly uses the word in bold, write *C* on the line below it. If a sentence is incorrect, rewrite it so that the vocabulary word in bold is used correctly.

1. An **icon** is a painting of a religious subject.

_____

atrophy

efficacy

emolument

icon

incipient

inculcate

inestimable

lackluster

martinet

prodigious

regimen

stellar

stoic

vibrant

zealous

2. To **inculcate** an idea is to teach it by frequently repeating it.

_____

3. A **regimen** is a military unit.

_____

4. A **zealous** person is one who shows an eager desire to achieve a goal.

_____

5. An **emolument** is a soothing cream or ointment.

_____

6. A **stellar** performance is one that cannot be improved upon.

7. A **vibrant** sound is one that is too loud.

8. A **martinet** is an award for a winning performance.

9. An **efficacious** medicine yields a therapeutic result.

10. To **atrophy** is to commit a terrible act.

11. Something of **inestimable** worth is too valuable to be measured.

12. A **prodigious** enterprise is one that excites wonder.

13. An **incipient** plan is one that fails to excite any interest.

14. A **stoic** attitude is one that regards risk-taking as pleasurable.

15. A **lackluster** stock market is one that has little vitality.

3B Using Words

If the word (or a form of the word) in bold fits in a sentence in the group below it, write the word in the blank. If the word does not fit, leave the space empty.

1. **regimen**

(a) The _____ marched past the grandstand, the colonel at its head.

(b) Her daily _____ includes a five-mile run and a low-fat, high-protein diet.

(c) The military _____ that ruled Greece was overthrown in 1974.

2. **vibrant**

(a) Your photograph captures perfectly the _____ colors of sugar maples in the fall.

(b) The _____ young couple drew admiring glances from passers-by.

(c) A long, pure, _____ note ended the soprano's solo.

3. **inculcate**

(a) Plants _____ moisture through their root systems.

(b) He is a teacher who is able to _____ a love of learning in his students.

(c) Doctors _____ children against diseases by various vaccines.

4. **lackluster**

(a) Her _____ response to the lecture suggests a lack of interest in geography.

(b) Joe can improve his _____ grades with a little extra effort.

(c) "Make your dog's _____ coat shine again with Shampooch," the label read.

5. **efficacy**

(a) Penicillin's _____ in treating infections has been known for several decades.

(b) The _____ of peacekeeping forces was put to the test in Bosnia.

(c) The _____ of television in aiding a political campaign is unquestioned.

6. **inestimable**

(a) Her _____ remark just before she hung up the phone left me feeling puzzled.

(b) The value of a painting like Vermeer's *The Goldweigher* is _____ .

(c) Think for a moment of the _____ distances between the galaxies.

7. **prodigious**

(a) I was disconcerted by the _____ looks I received from my fellow passenger.

(b) Picasso's _____ output amazes students of his work.

(c) Baryshnikov's _____ leaps made him a favorite of ballet lovers.

atrophy
efficacy
emolument
icon
incipient
inculcate
inestimable
lackluster
martinet
prodigious
regimen
stellar
stoic
vibrant
zealous

8. **zealous**

(a) "The secret of success," the speaker asserted, "is the _____ pursuit of excellence."

(b) Elizabeth Cady Stanton was a _____ advocate of women's rights.

(c) The _____ colors of the waving banners were dazzling to the eye.

3C Word Study

Complete the analogies by selecting the pair of words whose relationship most resembles the relationship of the pair of capital letters. Circle the letter in front of the pair you choose.

1. EMBARRASSED : MORTIFIED ::
   (a) untrue : apocryphal   (c) vibrant : patrician
   (b) shy : imperturbable   (d) angry : choleric

2. GESTICULATE : HAND ::
   (a) report : martinet   (c) nod : head
   (b) uproot : weed   (d) make : request

3. SUBTERFUGE : DECEIVE ::
   (a) icon : play   (c) obstacle : overcome
   (b) legacy : inherit   (d) antic : amuse

4. LEVITY : GRAVE ::
   (a) serenity : anxious   (c) fear : alarming
   (b) happiness : incipient   (d) apathy : indifferent

5. DISCONCERTED : COMPOSURE ::
   (a) wealthy : money   (c) angry : patience
   (b) hungry : appetite   (d) modest : zealous

6. PATRICIAN : CLASS ::
   (a) triangular : shape   (c) brave : soldier
   (b) lackluster : sunset   (d) readable : book

7. OPULENCE : IMPOVERISHED ::
   (a) calm : imperturbable   (c) star : stellar
   (b) levity : amusing   (d) destitution : rich

8. MARTINET : OBEY ::
   (a) doctor : heal   (c) student : learn
   (b) clown : amuse   (d) leader : follow

9. STOIC : PHLEGMATIC ::
   (a) subterfuge : lackluster   (c) raconteur : silent
   (b) sage : wise   (d) lesson : arcane

10. STELLAR : STAR ::

    (a) apocryphal : truth   (c) solar : sun

    (b) opulence : wealth   (d) central : periphery

3D Images of Words

Circle the letter of each sentence that suggests the numbered bold vocabulary word. In each group, you may circle more than one letter or none at all.

1. martinet

(a) The slightest inattentiveness brought a rap on the knuckles from Mr. Day.

(b) The new recruits dreaded the drill sergeant's approach.

(c) The house martin returned to the nest to feed her chicks.

2. regimen

(a) I start the day with three dozen push-ups and sit-ups.

(b) The recently elected government negotiated a settlement to the labor dispute.

(c) Every day at five o'clock, Delia took her seat at Tricolore Restaurant.

3. icon

(a) Within a few years of his death, Elvis Presley's grave had become a shrine.

(b) A cigarette with a diagonal line across it means "No Smoking."

(c) A painting of a Russian Orthodox bishop was on the magazine cover.

4. emolument

(a) Rubbing the cream into the aching joint brought much-needed relief.

(b) I asked Arlene when she could repay the loan I had made her.

(c) The position has a generous pension plan and full medical insurance.

5. vibrant

(a) The red and yellow shapes in Morandi's still life rested on a pale green plate.

(b) The studio lights were so strong they hurt my eyes.

(c) A huge explosion rocked the building.

6. zealous

(a) The manager scrutinized every report, searching for the slightest error.

(b) The puppy leaped up and down with delight when we returned home.

(c) My friend was nicknamed "Gusto Gretchen" for the way she played basketball.

7. atrophy

(a) Ms. Robinsky's children take almost no interest in the family business.

(b) Damaged nerves are slowly causing James to lose the use of his hand.

(c) Political freedoms can be lost gradually, leaving a society vulnerable to dictatorship.

atrophy
efficacy
emolument
icon
incipient
inculcate
inestimable
lackluster
martinet
prodigious
regimen
stellar
stoic
vibrant
zealous

8. **incipient**

   (a) Sniffles and sneezes may mean that you are coming down with the flu.

   (b) The isolated outbreaks of violence soon led to widespread civil unrest.

   (c) I was in the middle of my evening meal when the phone rang.

9. **stoic**

   (a) Phoebe didn't even grimace when the surgeon stitched her wound.

   (b) Walt stared blankly at the wall.

   (c) It was brave of Liza to order those bullies out of the room.

10. **stellar**

   (a) The light from a star can be analyzed to show the gases it contains.

   (b) Graf played great tennis, defeating her opponent 6–2, 7–5.

   (c) Jupiter has four large moons and a number of smaller ones.

3E Passage

Read the passage below; then complete the exercise that follows it.

No Excuses

When Wilma Rudolph was born on June 23, 1940, she weighed only four and a half pounds and had an **incipient** form of polio, a once-common disease that can cause paralysis and even death. As an infant, she was frequently ill. Her mother cared for her at home because there was only one doctor in their segregated town of Clarksville, Tennessee, who would treat black patients. By the time she was four, Wilma had contracted both double pneumonia and scarlet fever. In her weakened state, she was left vulnerable to the polio virus, which caused the muscles in her leg to **atrophy**. It seemed unlikely that she would ever walk normally again.

On the advice of her doctor, Rudolph began a weekly **regimen** of heat and water therapy at a Nashville hospital, some fifty miles from Clarksville. Mrs. Rudolph saw to it that her daughter exercised and received leg massages at home four times daily. Rudolph practiced her exercises **zealously**, despite constant pain. The treatments proved **efficacious**; at age five Wilma was fitted with a steel leg brace and took her first unsteady steps. With effort, she learned to walk; all the while despising the brace that set her apart from other children. While Wilma was **stoic** about her hardships, she was determined that someday she would walk without help.

As she worked toward this goal, the constant encouragement she received from her parents was of **inestimable** value. She was also fortunate in having a remarkable fourth-grade teacher, Mrs. Hoskins. Although something of a **martinet**, this woman was fair, treating everybody equally. She **inculcated** in her students the idea that they should think positively about their lives and their goals. "Do it, don't daydream about it," she would say. "No excuses!" Rudolph drew strength from this strong-minded teacher and her ideas. At age nine, she appeared in public without her brace for the first time. "From that day on," she later wrote, "people were going to . . . start thinking about me differently, start saying that Wilma is a healthy kid just like the rest of them." By the time she was eleven, she would no longer need to wear the brace.

Wilma demonstrated just how healthy she was in the seventh grade as a member of the school basketball team. Her speed and long arms and legs reminded her coach of a mosquito. He nicknamed her Skeeter, saying, "You're little, you're fast, and you always get in my way." Later she joined the school track team, where her gift for running became apparent. In an Amateur Athletic Union meet in Philadelphia, Rudolph won all of her nine races. Her **stellar** accomplishments on the track soon attracted national attention. At age sixteen, Wilma Rudolph became the youngest member of the United States Olympic track team, competing in the 1956

Melbourne Games. She gave what she considered a **lackluster** performance, winning a bronze medal in the 400-meter relay. She vowed to do better in the 1960 Olympics, to be held in Rome.

At the Olympic trials for the 1960 Games, Rudolph set a world record in the 200-meter dash. She also qualified for the 100-meter dash and the 400-meter relay. Only a few years after discarding the leg brace, she had become a tall, **vibrant** woman on the verge of her greatest triumph. But shortly after arriving in Rome for the Games, she stepped in a hole and twisted her ankle; it became swollen and discolored. It was at this point that the **prodigious** willpower that had served her so well in the past was again called into service. Despite the injury, Wilma competed, winning gold medals in all three of her events. She became the first woman to do so in the history of Olympic track and field.

In 1962, she retired from track. She said that she quit because, "I couldn't top what I did, so I'll be remembered for when I was at my best." She became a teacher and a coach. In the early 1960s few big corporations offered the **emoluments** that would make millionaires of sports heroes in the decades to follow. Wilma Rudolph never became wealthy, but her achievements on and off the track made her an **icon** to other athletes, to women, to African Americans, and to people with physical disabilities. Everyone can draw strength from her example and find inspiration in her story.

Answer each of the following questions in the form of a sentence. If a question does not contain a vocabulary word from this lesson's word list, use one in your answer. Use each word only once.

1. What details in the passage suggest that Wilma Rudolph's mother was a **vibrant** woman?

_____

2. How do you know that Wilma Rudolph was very interested in being able to walk?

_____

3. What details from the passage suggest that Wilma Rudolph did not complain about her situation?

_____

atrophy

efficacy

emolument

icon

incipient

inculcate

inestimable

lackluster

martinet

prodigious

regimen

stellar

stoic

vibrant

zealous

4. Why did Rudolph show no symptoms of polio as a baby?

_____

5. How did polio affect Rudolph's ability to walk?

_____

6. With what **regimen** did Rudolph's mother supplement the therapy provided by the hospital?

_____

7. How do you know that the efforts people made to help Rudolph were **efficacious**?

_____

8. In what way might the lessons that Mrs. Hoskins **inculcated** in fourth grade have helped Rudolph in Rome?

9. Why would it be inaccurate to describe Wilma Rudolph's performance in the 1960 Olympics as **lackluster**?

10. How might Rudolph's running career have been different if she had competed one or two decades later?

11. What do you think made Wilma Rudolph an **icon**?

12. The passage says Wilma Rudolph became a teacher and a coach. Do you think she would have been a **martinet** with her students? Explain your answer.

FUN & FASCINATING FACTS

Few people have had the honor (or misfortune) of contributing their names to the English language. Among this select group is Jean Martinet, a seventeenth-century French army officer. He was a strict disciplinarian who demanded rigid adherence to army rules. French words passing into English often retain their original pronunciation, and proper names usually remain capitalized. However, **martinet** breaks these rules; it does not require a capital *m* and is pronounced märt´n et´ instead of the French märt´n ā´.

Payments to millers for grinding corn in medieval England were called **emoluments**, from the Latin *molere*, "to grind." This word was later extended to payments of other kinds. *Molars*, the word for teeth that grind up food, comes from the same root.

The Greek word *stoa* meant "porch" and forms the root of **stoic**. Why this seemingly odd connection? The Greek philosopher Zeno (334–262 B.C.) taught that people should be free from passionate attachments and should accept whatever befalls them, for good or ill, with equal detachment. Because he customarily addressed his followers from the porch of his house, they became known as Stoics and his philosophy as Stoicism.

Lesson 4

Word List
Study the definitions of the words below; then do the exercises for the lesson.

autonomy
ô tän´ ə mē

n. The quality or state of being self-governing; independence.
Quebec's separatist movement seeks **autonomy** for the province.
autonomous *adj.*
Even though the think tank was located in the corporation's headquarters, it was an **autonomous** entity.

circumspect
sur´ kəm spekt

adj. Cautious and prudent; heedful of consequences.
A **circumspect** investor researches carefully before buying shares of any stock.

composure
kəm pō´ zhər

n. Calmness of mind or bearing; self-control.
Savanna maintained her **composure**, despite the prosecutor's repeated verbal attacks.

edifice
ed´ ə fis

n. 1. A large, imposing structure or building.
The **edifice** with the grand staircase is the Metropolitan Museum of Art.
2. A complex structure or system built up over time, as if it were a real building.
Successive generations of scholars have added to the **edifice** of science.

ensconce
en skäns´

v. To settle or place securely or snugly.
Grandfather **ensconced** himself in the armchair by the fire and promptly fell asleep.

environs
en vī´ rənz

n. The area adjoining or surrounding a place.
The combined population of Dayton, Ohio, and its **environs** exceeds two hundred thousand.

hapless
hap´ ləs

adj. Marked by the absence of good luck; unfortunate.
Ted's failed lawn-care service was merely the latest of his **hapless** ventures.

heinous
hā´ nəs

adj. Shockingly evil or wicked.
The execution of innocent civilians is a **heinous** act, even in times of war.

incognito
in käg nē´ tō

adj. or *adv.* With one's identity concealed; unrecognized.
The princess traveled **incognito** so that people would not recognize her.

indoctrinate
in däk´ trə nāt

v. 1. To teach or train in the fundamentals.
The Americorps volunteers were **indoctrinated** for several weeks before receiving an assignment.
2. To instill or teach from a partisan point of view.
The sergeant **indoctrinated** new recruits into the army's way of doing things.
indoctrination *n.*
The first-year law students received a thorough **indoctrination** into the rudiments of jurisprudence.

interim
in´ tər im

n. An interval of time between events.
I start my full-time job in May, but I'm looking for part-time work in the **interim**.
adj. Belonging to or taking place between events; temporary.
The **interim** peace treaty will be in force until a final agreement is negotiated.

mausoleum mô sə lē´ əm	*n.* A large and impressive tomb. The marble **mausoleum** holds the remains of Ulysses S. Grant.
pillage pil´ ij	*v.* To rob and plunder. After the army retreated, enemy troops **pillaged** the town, looting house after house.
reverie rev´ ər ē	*n.* 1. The condition of being lost in thought. With his work lying untouched before him, Carlos found himself in a **reverie** about the woman he loved. 2. A daydream. My **reveries** took me back to my mother's kitchen and the tantalizing smell of her turkey soup.
thrall thrôl	*n.* A loss of one's ability to act freely; a state over which one appears to have no control. Persons in **thrall** to tobacco find it difficult to break the addiction. **thralldom** *n.* Slavery or bondage. During the nineteenth century, the **thralldom** of Russian serfs kept them bound in service to the great landowners.

4A Understanding Meanings

Read the sentences below. If a sentence correctly uses the word in bold, write *C* on the line below it. If a sentence is incorrect, rewrite it so that the vocabulary word in bold is used correctly.

1. **Thralldom** is the state of being enslaved.

_____

2. An **interim** period is one that comes between two others.

_____

3. A **hapless** individual is one who doesn't have good luck.

_____

4. An **edifice** is an elaborate conceptual structure.

_____

5. To **pillage** an area is to use it to grow crops.

_____

6. To **ensconce** oneself is to settle in comfortably.

_____

7. An **autonomous** group is one that lacks purpose or direction.

8. A **reverie** is a feeling of deep respect.

9. **Indoctrination** is the inculcating of a set of ideas or beliefs.

10. A **heinous** act is one of prodigious wickedness.

11. The **environs** of a city are the amenities it offers.

12. A **circumspect** person is one with a propensity for taking risks.

13. To be **incognito** is to be without the means to support oneself.

14. **Composure** is calmness of manner.

autonomy
circumspect
composure
edifice   15. A **mausoleum** is a powerful political organization.
ensconce
environs
hapless
heinous   ## 4B Using Words
incognito
indoctrinate   If the word (or a form of the word) in bold fits a sentence in
interim   the group below it, write the word in the blank space. If the
mausoleum   word does not fit, leave the space empty.
pillage
reverie   1. **heinous**
thrall
                 (a) I told Marjorie she looked _____ with such heavy makeup.

                 (b) Under federal law, the death penalty is reserved for the most _____ crimes.

                 (c) I could tell from the _____ look Jeff gave me just what he thought of today's lunch.

2. **interim**

   (a) The _____ between the original price and the sale price was not that great.

   (b) Keesha Adams was named _____ treasurer until the next election.

   (c) During the short _____ between jobs, Maribel took care of her niece.

3. **pillage**

   (a) The Vikings descended on coastal villages to _____ and destroy.

   (b) Woodchucks _____ the neighborhood gardens in search of food.

   (c) Dr. Arias changed the _____ of his patient's medication.

4. **autonomous**

   (a) Non-native species are replacing the fauna that is _____ to the region.

   (b) In 1781, thirteen _____ states joined together to form a Republic.

   (c) Each school district is _____ and is not subject to state or federal control.

5. **environs**

   (a) Air pollution concerns people who care about the global _____ .

   (b) The city and its _____ occupy twenty-five square miles.

   (c) Using Bordeaux as our base, we spent three or four days exploring the _____ .

6. **mausoleum**

   (a) An iron railing surrounded the late emperor's granite _____ .

   (b) Miss Havisham's gloomy house seemed like a _____ to young Pip.

   (c) The body was borne to its grave on a _____ carried by six mourners.

7. **indoctrinate**

   (a) Infants are _____ against a variety of childhood diseases.

   (b) It is the job of the personnel manager to _____ the new employees in company policy.

   (c) Rasheed was thrilled when he was _____ into the college honor society.

8. **circumspect**

   (a) A _____ person always looks before she leaps.

   (b) Some wealthy businesspeople find ways to _____ the tax laws.

   (c) It is best to be _____ before taking any drastic action.

4C Word Study

Fill in the missing word in each of the sentences below. Then write a brief definition of the word. The number in parentheses gives the lesson from which the word is taken.

1. The Latin *stella* means "star." It forms the English word _____ (3), meaning _____ .

2. The prefix *auto-* means "self." It combines with the Latin *nomos* (the law) to form the English word _____ (4), meaning _____ .

3. The prefix *inter-* means "between." It combines with the Latin *ponere* (to put) to form the English word _____ (2), meaning _____ .

4. The prefix *con-* means "together." It combines with the Latin *venire* (to come) to form the English word _____ (1), meaning _____ .

5. The prefix *in-* often means "not." It combines with the Latin *cognitus* (known) to form the English word _____ (4), meaning _____ .

6. The prefix *a-* means "without." It combines with the Greek *trophe* (food) to form the English word _____ (3), meaning _____ .

7. The prefix *circum-* means "around." It combines with the Latin *specere* (to look) to form the English word _____ (4), meaning _____ .

8. The Latin *levis* means "light." It forms the English word _____ (1), meaning _____ .

9. The Latin *utilas* means "useful." It forms the English word _____ (2), meaning _____ .

10. The prefix *apo-* means "away from." It combines with the Greek *kruptein* (to hide) to form the English word _____ (1), meaning _____ .

autonomy
circumspect
composure
edifice
ensconce
environs
hapless
heinous
incognito
indoctrinate
interim
mausoleum
pillage
reverie
thrall

4D Images of Words

Circle the letter of each sentence that suggests the numbered bold vocabulary word. In each group, you may circle more than one letter or none at all.

1. **composure**

   (a) Mozart wrote this symphony when he was only seven years old.

   (b) Fred ignored the taunts of his classmates, and they soon left him alone.

   (c) The sun is made up of hydrogen, helium, and a few trace elements.

2. **hapless**

   (a) The fishermen were adrift and out of sight of land, with dark clouds massing overhead.

   (b) After the monitor told us to open our test booklets, we were on our own.

   (c) Survivors of the earthquake were unaware of the approaching tidal wave.

3. **indoctrinate**

   (a) The first lesson that medical students are taught is "Do no harm."

   (b) She claims to be without religious beliefs of any kind.

   (c) The grand jury charged the suspect with armed robbery.

4. **autonomy**

   (a) The vivid colors of the leaves told us that fall had arrived.

   (b) A feature of this camera is its ability to rewind the film as soon as the final picture is taken.

   (c) There is no bridge to the island, which must be reached by boat.

5. **incognito**

   (a) The identity of the poem's author is not known.

   (b) The film star registered at the hotel under the name Marilyn Rodriguez.

   (c) Astronauts traveling on the moon's far side were cut off from all communication.

6. **thralldom**

   (a) The children couldn't take their eyes off the magician as he opened the large wooden box.

   (b) For hundreds of years, enslaved Africans performed hard labor in the Americas.

   (c) Janet's infatuation with tennis occupied her thoughts every waking moment.

7. **reverie**

   (a) The sound of the bugle awoke the campers from their deep slumber.

   (b) Theo was staring at the mountains, oblivious to everything I had said.

   (c) Those who frequented Judge Bell's courtroom developed a deep respect for her.

8. **ensconce**

   (a) The president's favorite spot was in the comfortable rocking chair he made famous.

   (b) The vase was in its usual place, in a niche on the wall of the dining room.

   (c) With a batting average of .395, Aaron's place on the team was secure.

9. **edifice**

   (a) She lives in the small brick house on that street corner.

   (b) Buckingham Palace is a popular tourist attraction for visitors to London.

   (c) The media empire the partners had built up over four decades collapsed overnight.

10. **circumspect**

    (a) Hilda opened the box very carefully, as though she expected to find a slithering reptile.

    (b) Charles checked the safety record of the airline before he booked his flight.

    (c) Working with great care, Elsie made a drawing of her two cats at play.

4E Passage

Read the passage below; then complete the exercise that follows it.

Tibet's God-King?

The thirteenth Dalai Lama was not simply the head of the government of Tibet. Like his predecessors, he was revered as a god-king—as the reincarnation of the Buddha of Compassion—by the Buddhist people of that fascinating land. When he died in 1933, they believed that his soul would enter the body of a child, who would in time become the next Dalai Lama. In strict accordance with ancient Tibetan tradition, a high Buddhist monk was appointed to rule Tibet as regent during this **interim** period. One day, the regent fell into a **reverie** during which he saw where the new Dalai Lama would be found. He described in detail both the house and its **environs**. Search parties set out to look for the place and the child, the first step in a time-honored procedure for seeking, locating, and training the new leader of Tibet.

In the summer of 1937, after the officials had covered over a thousand miles and had interviewed several candidates, they received promising details about a two-year-old boy living in the province of Amdo in northeastern Tibet. High government officials, traveling **incognito**, stopped at his house for a visit. The place where the boy lived precisely matched the regent's description. As a test, the officials showed the boy several pairs of objects. One item of each pair had belonged to the former Dalai Lama; the other was an identical copy. When asked to choose between them, the boy invariably rejected the copies. The officials were satisfied that the long search for the new incarnation of their leader was over.

Tibet is bounded by the Himalaya Mountains to the south and west and by desert to the north and east. It is not easily accessible to the outside world. For this reason, Lhasa, its capital, was long known as the "Forbidden City." Built into a towering rock face overlooking Lhasa is an imposing **edifice** known as the Potala Palace. More than a quarter of a mile long, filled with thousands of rooms, halls, and chapels connected by narrow corridors, this huge building can become dark and gloomy. In the winter when it is bitterly cold, it can seem more like a **mausoleum** than a residence. The little boy was **ensconced** in an apartment within the palace and began the training program that would prepare him to be the country's spiritual leader. After three years he was installed as the fourteenth Dalai Lama in an elaborate and lengthy ceremony. Those who witnessed the events remarked on the five-year-old's grave manner and perfect **composure**.

autonomy
circumspect
composure
edifice
ensconce
environs
hapless
heinous
incognito
indoctrinate
interim
mausoleum
pillage
reverie
thrall

To the north and east of Tibet is China. Over the centuries, the government of Tibet had learned to be **circumspect** in dealing with its powerful neighbor. China had long claimed Tibet as a Chinese province but had allowed it to maintain **autonomy**. In 1949, however, China came under Communist rule, and one year later the Chinese army invaded Tibet on eight separate fronts. The **hapless** Tibetan army was swept aside; its soldiers were outnumbered, ill-trained, poorly armed, and, as devout Buddhists, had learned to oppose the taking of all life. The Dalai Lama was forced to agree that Tibet was officially a Chinese province. In return, he was promised that there would be no change in his status and powers. That promise was soon broken.

Communist leaders in Beijing outlawed religion in China and would not tolerate a province where almost a third of the men were monks and where Buddhism dominated every aspect of the people's lives. Chairman Mao promised to "liberate" the Tibetan people from the **thralldom** of religion. The Tibetan people were never asked whether or not they wanted such "liberation."

Chinese soldiers began the systematic destruction of the religious and cultural institutions of Tibet. They **pillaged** the monasteries, stripping them of all treasures, which were sent to China to be sold. The thousands of monks who resisted were shot. Only a few of Tibet's more than 6,000 monasteries, temples, and libraries survived intact. Tibetan youths were sent to China for Communist **indoctrination**, while the rest of the population was organized into forced labor groups. Chinese settlers entered the country and took up residence.

In March of 1959, when it appeared that Chinese officials were planning to take the Dalai Lama into custody, he fled to northern India where he established a government-in-exile. By the end of the year, nearly eight thousand Tibetan refugees had joined him. Since that time he has worked tirelessly to return Tibet to its earlier state of independence. He travels around the world, telling all who will listen of the **heinous** crimes committed against his people and advocating peaceful means of resolving political conflicts. He was awarded the 1989 Nobel Peace Prize in recognition of his nonviolent campaign to end Chinese domination of Tibet. Whether he and his followers will ever return to their homeland is difficult to foresee, yet clearly the Dalai Lama remains a powerful symbol of Tibet's lost independence. If in the end he cannot return, the fourteenth Dalai Lama may well be the last.

Answer each of the following questions in the form of a sentence. If a question does not contain a vocabulary word from this lesson's word list, use one in your answer. Use each word only once.

1. In what way were the officials **circumspect** in their search for the next Dalai Lama?

2. What evidence seems to show that the child Dalai Lama felt comfortable in his new **environs**?

3. What **indoctrination** did the Dalai Lama receive when he was a child?

4. Is the Potala Palace a **mausoleum**? Explain your answer.

5. How did the **reverie** of the regent help to locate the next Dalai Lama?

6. Why would it be inaccurate to describe the invading Chinese soldiers as **hapless**?

7. Is it accurate to say that the Dalai Lama remained the ruler of Tibet from 1949 to 1959? Explain your answer.

8. Why is "liberate" put in quotation marks in reference to Mao's promise?

9. What are some of the **heinous** crimes perpetrated against Tibet?

10. Why did the Dalai Lama **ensconce** himself in northern India in 1959?

11. What is the present political status of the Tibetan people?

12. What do you think is the exiled Dalai Lama's dearest wish?

FUN & FASCINATING FACTS

Circumspect is formed from the Latin prefix *circum-*, "around," and the root from the Latin verb *specere*, "to look." A person who rushes into something without first looking around is not being circumspect. What other words with the root "specere" come to mind?

Mausolus was a minor ruler of the kingdom of Caria, in what is now Turkey, who would long ago have been forgotten were it not for his wife Artemisia. On his death in 353 B.C., she had built for him a magnificent tomb encased in marble that was supposedly 411 feet in circumference and 140 feet tall. This **mausoleum**, so named for the dead king, was one of the seven wonders of the ancient world. The word eventually came to refer to any large tomb.

Review for Lessons 1–4

Crossword Puzzle Solve the crossword puzzle below by studying the clues and filling in the answer boxes. Clues followed by a number are definitions of words in Lessons 1 through 4. The number gives the word list in which the answer to the clue appears.

Clues Across

2. A loss of the ability to act freely (4)
7. To waste away or fail to develop (3)
10. To roam about, plundering (2)
11. An increase, addition, or gain (1)
12. Oslo is the capital of this country
13. One who suffers without complaining (3)
18. Self-government (4)
20. A symbol or image (3)
23. To flow out slowly (1)
24. Columbus is the capital of this state
25. Understood by only a few (1)
28. To put between two things (2)
29. The holy book of the religion of Islam
30. A program to maintain health (3)
32. Of or related to a star (3)
33. Having or exhibiting richness (2)

Clues Down

1. To be unable to make up one's mind (1)
2. Tenth president of the United States
3. A lack of seriousness (1)
4. Animals of a particular region (2)
5. Showing refinement of taste (2)
6. Famed American writer _____ Allan Poe
8. A skilled storyteller (1)
9. A small amount (2)
14. An interval of time between events (4)
15. Famed baseball player _____ Cobb
16. Feeling injury or offense (2)
17. With one's identity concealed (4)
19. A strict disciplinarian (3)
21. To embarrass or humiliate (1)
22. Full of life or vigor (3)
26. Mistakes
27. A group of three
31. Opposite of "well"

Lesson 5

> ## Word List
Study the definitions of the words below; then do the exercises for the lesson.

abstruse
əb strōōs´

adj. Difficult to understand.
The professor's circuitous explanation of how to solve the problem was so **abstruse** that we had trouble following it.

accrue
ə krōō´

v. 1. To arise or increase as a natural result or growth, usually used with *to* or *from*.
Hubble's prodigious knowledge of astronomy **accrued** from years of studying the heavens.
2. To come as a regular addition.
Interest on the savings account **accrues** monthly.

acquiesce
ak wē es´

v. To accept as inevitable; to comply passively.
Marta felt obliged to **acquiesce** when her supervisor suggested that she work late.
acquiescence *n.*
The strikers demanded from management immediate **acquiescence** to their requests.

besmirch
bē smurch´

v. To stain or tarnish; to make dirty.
"The sole reason for the existence of tabloids," Amelia asserted, "is to **besmirch** the reputation of famous people."

explicit
ek splis´ it

adj. Fully and clearly expressed, leaving nothing merely implied.
The **explicit** directions made assembling the grill a simple task.

histrionic
his trē än´ ik

adj. Purposely affected; theatrical.
Minh's **histrionic** moans failed to convince the school nurse to send her home.
histrionics *n. pl.* Exaggerated displays of emotion, intended to produce an effect or response.
In an astonishing display of **histrionics**, Bart actually knelt and begged Vivian to accompany him to dinner.

impropriety
im prə prī´ ə tē

n. 1. The quality or state of being improper or unsuitable.
Dolores saw no **impropriety** in hiring her qualified friend for the job.
2. Something that is improper.
The senator was mortified when he was reprimanded for mishandling campaign contributions and for various other **improprieties**.

inveigle
in vā´ gəl

v. 1. To lure or trick into doing something.
By posing as a reporter, the agent **inveigled** the guard into letting her enter the complex.
2. To obtain by flattery or trickery.
By saying he had to pick up a friend, Mark **inveigled** the keys to Daniel's car.

penitent
pen´ i tənt

adj. Sorry for having done wrong.
Agatha was in a **penitent** state of mind after realizing that she had chastised her daughter unfairly.
penitence *n.*
As Bill returned with the stolen books, his **penitence** seemed genuine.

probity
prō´ bə tē

n. Honesty; trustworthiness; adherence to virtue.
A high level of **probity** is expected from workers who handle cash.

purport pər pôrt′	*v.* To give or present the often false impression of being someone or intending something. The woman **purports** to be a surviving member of the Russian royal family.
repercussion rē pər kush′ ən	*n.* An unforeseen or indirect result or effect of an event. Last fall's flooding of California farmland will have economic **repercussions** throughout the country.
revelation rev ə lā′ shən	*n.* Something that is made known or revealed, often coming as a surprise. Ms. Curran's knowledge of arcane points of property law was a **revelation** to me.
surfeit sur′ fit	*n.* An overabundant supply; an excess. The **surfeit** of evidence left the jury little room for doubt as to the suspect's guilt.
unsavory un sā′ vər ē	*adj.* 1. Having an unpleasant look, taste, or smell. The week-old sandwich had an **unsavory** aroma. 2. Morally offensive. More details of the **unsavory** scandal became known after the mayor assaulted his business partner.

5A Understanding Meanings

Read the sentences below. If a sentence correctly uses the word in bold, write *C* on the line below it. If a sentence is incorrect, rewrite it so that the vocabulary word in bold is used correctly.

1. **Penitence** is remorse for one's mistakes.

_____

2. An **explicit** statement is one whose meaning is clear.

_____

3. To **purport** an interest is to claim, perhaps falsely, to have one.

_____

4. **Repercussions** are sounds that echo.

_____

5. To **acquiesce** is to accept by not raising any objections.

_____

6. **Probity** is a period of suspended action.

_____

7. An **abstruse** passage is one that is not easy to understand.

8. An **unsavory** character offends one's moral sensibilities.

9. To **inveigle** a position is to obtain it through devious means.

10. **Histrionics** are written accounts of past occurrences.

11. To **accrue** is to come as a natural addition to something.

12. A **surfeit** of something is an oversupply of it.

13. To **besmirch** someone is to harass that person with requests.

14. **Impropriety** is the state of being unsuitable.

15. A **revelation** is a surprising disclosure.

abstruse
accrue
acquiesce
besmirch
explicit
histrionic
impropriety
inveigle
penitent
probity
purport
repercussion
revelation
surfeit
unsavory

5B Using Words

If the word (or a form of the word) in bold fits a sentence in the group below it, write the word in the blank space. If the word does not fit, leave the space empty.

1. **impropriety**

   (a) Using office stamps for your personal mail was a minor _____ .

   (b) Janet was appalled by the _____ of her English teacher's flirting with students.

   (c) "Of what _____ am I accused?" Meredith demanded indignantly.

2. **purport**

   (a) Those who _____ to uphold the law have an obligation not to break it.

   (b) Recent poll results _____ to show what the public is thinking about the president's performance.

   (c) "I _____ a toast to the bride and groom for long life and happiness."

3. **accrue**

   (a) Many advantages _____ to societies that have stable governments.

   (b) Penalties on unpaid taxes _____ from the date they should have been paid.

   (c) Leaves _____ in the gutters of the roof and block the drainpipes.

4. **explicit**

   (a) I received _____ orders not to leave unless you came with me.

   (b) He attempted to set down in _____ detail a code of conduct for the colony.

   (c) The passage is so _____ that it leaves no room for misunderstanding.

5. **unsavory**

   (a) Avid readers devoured every _____ detail of the couple's divorce.

   (b) Those _____ acquaintances of yours may lead you into serious trouble.

   (c) Stale cigarette smoke left an _____ smell in the car's interior.

6. **inveigle**

   (a) Mary _____ her way backstage and marched right into the star's dressing room.

   (b) The partners _____ Josh into putting up all the money for their project.

   (c) Through flattery, they _____ a promise from Charlayne that she would appear at the tryouts.

7. **acquiesce**

   (a) Worn out by their repeated demands, Ford was finally obliged to _____ .

   (b) I think we can all _____ that no action is needed at this time.

   (c) Najah indicated her _____ by signing the paper they put before her.

8. **besmirch**

   (a) When Sam was convicted of embezzlement, he _____ his family's good name.

   (b) The artist _____ a broad brush stroke of crimson across the bare canvas.

   (c) The mud struck Giles on the chest and _____ his white shirt front.

5C Word Study

Each group of four words below contains two words that are either synonyms or antonyms. Circle these two words, then circle the *S* if they are synonyms, the *A* if they are antonyms.

1. strengthen	vacillate	atrophy	inculcate	S	A
2. circumspect	prodigious	incognito	audacious	S	A
3. arcane	opulent	abstruse	histrionic	S	A
4. penitent	prodigious	efficacious	puny	S	A
5. heinous	onerous	hapless	commendable	S	A
6. submit	accrue	acquiesce	inculcate	S	A
7. efficacious	effective	stoic	apocryphal	S	A
8. autonomous	phlegmatic	fortunate	hapless	S	A
9. accumulate	comport	purport	accrue	S	A
10. utilitarian	lackluster	credible	vibrant	S	A

5D Images of Words

Circle the letter of each sentence that suggests the numbered bold vocabulary word. In each group, you may circle more than one letter or none at all.

1. **histrionics**

   (a) John Jay was the first chief justice of the United States Supreme Court.

   (b) Crashes are staged by the auto company to test the efficacy of the air bags.

   (c) "I will never, ever clean my room again!" howled Arnie at the top of his lungs.

2. **penitence**

   (a) "Excuse me for a moment," signed Krystyna and slipped out of the room.

   (b) I am terribly sorry if my remark upset you, and I hope you will forgive me.

   (c) The faithful climbed the steps on their knees to show sorrow for their sins.

3. **revelation**

   (a) I had no idea that your Aunt Helen was a United States senator.

   (b) The birthday girl had known all along about the surprise party her friends were planning.

   (c) I was amazed at how easily the XJ-32 handled on tight curves.

abstruse
accrue
acquiesce
besmirch
explicit
histrionic
impropriety
inveigle
penitent
probity
purport
repercussion
revelation
surfeit
unsavory

4. **unsavory**

   (a) Annette mistakenly added a bottle of vinegar to the stew.

   (b) By the time I had finished cleaning the greasy pans, the dishwater looked very unappealing.

   (c) The man's shifty look made me circumspect in my dealings with him.

5. **acquiescence**

   (a) By Thursday, the floodwaters had subsided to a normal level.

   (b) We were in complete agreement on the terms of the contract.

   (c) The waitress escorted us to our usual table.

6. **abstruse**

   (a) Boolean algebra is a mathematical construct used in computer science.

   (b) Quantum mechanics explains the structure and behavior of atoms.

   (c) I had difficulty with the irregular verbs on today's French test.

7. **impropriety**

   (a) The accident was caused by a poorly installed safety latch.

   (b) Although he committed no crime, Warren showed poor judgment.

   (c) Each child gave Ms. Ruiz a gift upon her retirement from teaching.

8. **probity**

   (a) For over forty years, Wallace Appliance Store has fulfilled its service contracts completely.

   (b) The Mariner spacecraft was designed to probe the atmosphere of Venus.

   (c) She had lived to be ninety, she said, because she walked several miles almost every day.

9. **repercussion**

   (a) Charlie started to play the drums before he was even five.

   (b) No one really knows what the consequences of the new law will be.

   (c) The teacher, being out of the room, did not see his students throwing paper airplanes.

10. **surfeit**

   (a) His indigestion was caused by eating too many fried clams.

   (b) For a millionaire to win twenty million dollars is too much of a good thing.

   (c) The supply of oil exceeded the demand, which explains the recent drop in price.

5E Passage

Read the passage below; then complete the exercise that follows it.

The Quiz-Show Scandal

Sponsors, who pay considerable sums of money to advertise their products on network television, are not permitted to dictate the content of the shows during which their commercials run. Their role is strictly limited to deciding on which shows they will purchase commercial time. This has not always been the case. A major change in the relationship between commercial sponsors and programs was triggered in the 1950s by one of television's most **unsavory** episodes—the quiz-show scandal. Its **repercussions** are felt to this day.

Early television producers often looked to the well-established medium of radio for ideas on which to base their shows. Thus, the *$64 Question*, which had been popular on radio, became a weekly television program renamed *The $64,000 Question*. Contestants on this show were asked simple questions at the start, which became more **abstruse** as the dollar amount for a correct answer increased. Successful contestants returned week after week, with their winnings **accruing** until they reached $64,000, the top prize and an enormous sum at the time.

The program quickly became the most popular show on television. Before long there was a **surfeit** of big-money quiz shows on the air. Because competition for viewers was intense, many shows were not the simple tests of knowledge they **purported** to be.

Producers came under intense pressure from their sponsors and from the networks to be certain that the shows were as dramatic and entertaining as possible to draw more viewers and to gain higher ratings. The viewers were **inveigled** into thinking that contestants were hearing the questions for the first time. In fact, the contestants had been coached on the questions beforehand. Their furrowed brows and anguished looks as they tried to think of the correct answers were carefully rehearsed **histrionics**.

A young lecturer from Columbia University named Charles Van Doren was one of those contestants on a quiz show called *Twenty-One*. Van Doren, who came from a distinguished American literary family that included a Pulitzer Prize–winning poet, was impressed by the fact that the show glorified knowledge rather than athletics or show business. There were no **improprieties** when Van Doren first discussed appearing on the show, but soon he was drawn into a web of deception as the producers' hints about questions and answers became more **explicit**. When they dropped all pretense and offered him a chance to see the questions before each show, he at first indignantly rejected the proposal, but in the end weakened and **acquiesced**. Van Doren was persuaded that if he won and kept winning, he would help make this show about knowledge as exciting as those showing crime and violence.

Too many people knew that the show was fixed for it to remain a secret for very long. The suspicions of the New York district attorney were aroused enough for him to begin an investigation. The case exploded when a former contestant came to him with a devastating **revelation**. The contestant had been given the answers to questions that would be asked on *Twenty-One*. At first, Van Doren and others involved in the show indignantly denied the charges. They claimed their reputations were being **besmirched** by a former loser on the show, and a sore loser at that. The problem with the district attorney's case was that it was not actually illegal to feed contestants the right answers. Now it was time for Congress to get into the act. If there were no laws against rigging TV quiz shows, maybe there ought to be.

Congressional hearings were held, and those involved in *Twenty-One* and similar shows were forced to testify under oath and in the glare of the national spotlight. A now **penitent** Van Doren expressed his regret at deceiving the public, his friends, and his family. He was fired from his job as a consultant for NBC and resigned his teaching position at Columbia University.

Along with twenty other witnesses, Van Doren was charged with perjury for lying before the district attorney's grand jury. All received suspended sentences. As a result of the scandal, laws were passed that attempted to regulate the television industry, but the public's faith in the **probity** of those who ran television received a blow from which it never completely recovered.

abstruse
accrue
acquiesce
besmirch
explicit
histrionic
impropriety
inveigle
penitent
probity
purport
repercussion
revelation
surfeit
unsavory

After leaving Columbia, Van Doren worked for *Encyclopedia Britannica* and wrote numerous books including *A History of Knowledge: Past, Present and Future*. In June of 1999, an invitation from the Class of 1959 to speak at its reunion brought Charles Van Doren back to Columbia for only the second time in 40 years.

Answer each of the following questions in the form of a sentence. If a question does not contain a vocabulary word from this lesson's word list, use one in your answer. Use each word only once.

1. How did the success of *The $64,000 Question* bear out the truth of the saying that imitation is the sincerest form of flattery?

2. Why would the contestants have needed no help with questions in the early rounds?

3. Why was it necessary for the contestants to engage in **histrionics**?

4. How is it suggested that viewers believed the contestants' knowledge to be genuine?

5. When should Charles Van Doren have become suspicious and backed out?

6. Why might some contestants on *Twenty-One* be upset as they watched their opponents' winnings **accrue**?

7. What effect would **revelations** of cheating in a quiz show have on television viewers today? Explain your answer.

8. In your opinion, what did Charles Van Doren lose when he **acquiesced** to the producers' demands to cheat?

9. What was one of the more immediate **repercussions** of the scandal?

10. How did Charles Van Doren acknowledge the **impropriety** of what he had done?

11. Why might other teachers have particular reason to regard this episode in television history as **unsavory**?

FUN & FASCINATING FACTS

Abstract has several meanings; one of them is "difficult to understand," and in this sense it is synonymous with **abstruse**. It may be that people have ambivalent feelings about information that is difficult to understand—at least, the roots of the two words suggest as much. *Abstract* is formed from the Latin verb *abstrahere*, "to draw or drag away," while *abstruse* comes from the Latin verb *abstrudere*, "to push away."

Probity is formed from the Latin *probus*, "upright" or "good." (A person of probity can be trusted in any situation.) Several other words are derived from this root. A *proper* course of action is one that is good. *Approbation* is an expression of approval for upright behavior. Someone placed on *probation* is relieved of having to go to jail as long as that person maintains good behavior.

Lesson 6

Word List
Study the definitions of the words below; then do the exercises for the lesson.

anathema
ə na´ thə mə

n. Someone or something that is intensely disliked, cursed, or shunned.
Raising taxes was **anathema** to home owners who believed they were already paying more than their share.

assuage
ə swāj´

v. 1. To satisfy.
After the tennis match, my friend and I **assuaged** our thirst at a lemonade stand.
2. To lessen or reduce the intensity of.
A hug is sometimes all it takes to **assuage** a child's fears.

avuncular
ə vən´ kyə lər

adj. Like a benevolent uncle; familiar and indulgent.
Sid, an **avuncular** friend of my father, exuded goodwill and always presented us with charming little gifts when he visited.

convivial
kən viv´ ē əl

adj. Sociable; concerned with good company and festivities.
The Haddad family reunion was a **convivial** banquet, lasting far into the night.

eclectic
e klek´ tik

adj. Combining elements from a variety of sources.
We enjoyed the small, unpretentious restaurant whose **eclectic** menu offered Thai, Ethiopian, and Argentinian cuisine.

epigram
ep´ ə gram

n. A short, witty poem or saying.
I am reminded of Dr. Johnson's **epigram** that a second marriage is "the triumph of hope over experience."

expound
ek spound´

v. To explain in detail; to set forth.
Kareem **expounded** his religious beliefs while his friends listened intently.

intrinsic
in trin´ sik

adj. Relating to the essential nature of something; real or actual.
Although the crystal appeared to be a diamond, careful examination revealed that it had no **intrinsic** value.

inveterate
in vet´ ər ət

adj. Habitual or deeply rooted; persistent.
It goes without saying that good raconteurs are **inveterate** storytellers.

mogul
mō´ gəl

n. A very powerful or wealthy person; a magnate.
The two banking **moguls** met to discuss a merger that would give them dominance in the New England region.

munificent
myōō nif´ ə sənt

adj. Extremely generous; liberal in giving.
The basketball star's **munificent** donation completely funded the construction of the new community center.
munificence *n.*
The foundation was known for its **munificence** in endowing hospitals and research centers around the world.

nascent nā´ sənt	*adj.* Beginning to exist; emerging. The country's **nascent** economy, which had developed since the end of the war, was devastated by an earthquake.
perspicacious pʉr spi kā´ shəs	*adj.* Clear-sighted; shrewd. Realizing quickly that Randolph was **perspicacious** in investment matters, I relied on him for guidance. **perspicacity** *n.* Because of her many years of training and experience, the psychologist displayed **perspicacity** of judgment about her patients' psyches.
philistine fil´ i stēn	*n.* One who is indifferent to or disdainful of intellectual values. "It was the **philistines** on the school board," argued Mr. Winkler, "who cut the music department budget in order to transfer funds to the athletic department." *adj.* Smugly ignorant of artistic or intellectual qualities. The **philistine** proposal to close the art museum angered local residents.
propitious prō pish´ əs	*adj.* Tending to favor or assist; encouraging. Senator Feynman's sixty percent approval rating was a **propitious** start to her re-election effort.

6A Understanding Meanings

Read the sentences below. If a sentence correctly uses the word in bold, write *C* on the line below it. If a sentence is incorrect, rewrite it so that the vocabulary word in bold is used correctly.

1. To **expound** one's beliefs is to explain them in detail.

_____

2. A **nascent** trend is one that is well established.

_____

anathema

assuage

avuncular

convivial

eclectic

epigram

expound

intrinsic

inveterate

mogul

munificent

nascent

perspicacious

philistine

propitious

3. An **epigram** is a statement praising someone who has recently died.

_____

4. A **propitious** interview is one likely to bring good results.

_____

5. A **philistine** is a person who is indifferent to art and culture.

_____

6. A **munificent** gesture is one that is made grudgingly.

_____

7. An **intrinsic** quality is one that expresses the very nature of a thing.

8. A **mogul** is a creature that threatens or terrifies.

9. To **assuage** a thirst is to quench it.

10. **Perspicacity** is the ability to make sound judgments.

11. An **anathema** is a substance that causes unconsciousness.

12. A **convivial** gathering is one that is enjoyed by those attending it.

13. An **inveterate** habit is one that is firmly established.

14. An **eclectic** group is one whose members come from a variety of backgrounds.

15. An **avuncular** attitude is one that is resented for being condescending.

6B Using Words

If the word (or a form of the word) in bold fits a sentence in the group below it, write the word in the blank. If the word does not fit, leave the space empty.

1. **expound**

    (a) Football fans love to _____ on the merits of their favorite teams.

    (b) She was able to _____ a single paragraph into a six-page paper.

    (c) Despite widespread criticism, Ayn Rand continued to _____ her philosophy that greed is good.

2. **perspicacious**

    (a) Joanne's _____ made her a candidate for rapid promotion.

    (b) The extreme heat in the room was making the occupants visibly _____ .

    (c) The candidate's analysis of the situation was most _____ .

3. **assuage**

    (a) We had nothing in the refrigerator but a few leftovers with which to _____ our hunger.

    (b) Gentle massage will help to _____ the pain in your shoulder.

    (c) I'm sure that a word of apology will _____ your aunt's anger.

4. **eclectic**

    (a) The design of the house successfully combines an _____ mix of architectural details.

    (b) An _____ shock ran through the room when the announcement was made.

    (c) This semester, along with the required courses, I can take two _____ .

5. **propitious**

    (a) You could not have chosen a more _____ time to give me this information.

    (b) Conditions in the colonies were _____ for advocating independence.

    (c) Evening gowns and tuxedos are _____ dress for attending the gala opening.

6. **inveterate**

    (a) _____ gamblers find it very difficult to stop gaming even as their losses mount.

    (b) Regina tried to control the _____ distaste she felt toward her neighbor's dog.

    (c) The _____ police officers were usually paired with the rookies to show them the ropes.

7. **avuncular**

    (a) Stalin's _____ manner with close associates masked his cold-blooded nature.

    (b) For two dollars you can ride the _____ to the top of Mount Hollyburn.

    (c) Harriet disliked the _____ tone her boss often used with her.

8. **intrinsic**

    (a) These old family photographs have both sentimental and _____ value.

    (b) The _____ merit of some Saturday morning television is close to nil.

    (c) Lange's portraits often reveal the _____ nature of her subjects.

anathema

assuage

avuncular

convivial

eclectic

epigram

expound

intrinsic

inveterate

mogul

munificent

nascent

perspicacious

philistine

propitious

6C Word Study

Complete the analogies by selecting the pair of words whose relationship most resembles the relationship of the pair of capital letters. Circle the letter in front of the pair you choose.

1. BUILDING : EDIFICE ::
   - (a) book : tome
   - (b) brick : mortar
   - (c) munificent : philistine
   - (d) kitten : cat

2. TOMB : MAUSOLEUM ::
   - (a) mogul : convivial
   - (b) bike : bicycle
   - (c) house : mansion
   - (d) car : automobile

3. CITY : ENVIRONS ::
   - (a) surfeit : excess
   - (b) animal : fauna
   - (c) circle : shape
   - (d) center : periphery

4. MODICUM : SURFEIT ::
   - (a) increment : addition
   - (b) minimum : maximum
   - (c) reward : propitious
   - (d) payment : emolument

5. DRAMATIC : HISTRIONIC ::
   - (a) aggrieved : choleric
   - (b) lackluster : stellar
   - (c) serious : playful
   - (d) foolhardy : circumspect

6. FOREBODINGS : REPERCUSSIONS ::
   - (a) hopes : dreams
   - (b) premonitions : consequences
   - (c) memories : fears
   - (d) joys : sorrows

7. SORRY : PENITENT ::
   - (a) fervent : restrained
   - (b) choleric : therapeutic
   - (c) subdued : exuberant
   - (d) anxious : distraught

8. PROPITIOUS : INAUSPICIOUS ::
   - (a) optimistic : pessimistic
   - (b) spurious : bogus
   - (c) pernicious : harmful
   - (d) malicious : vicious

9. EPIGRAM : WITTY ::
   - (a) subterfuge : unsavory
   - (b) regimen : efficacious
   - (c) surfeit : abundant
   - (d) rumor : apocryphal

10. MOGUL : POWERFUL ::
   - (a) crime : heinous
   - (b) ruse : expedient
   - (c) martinet : strict
   - (d) edifice : opulent

6D Images of Words

Circle the letter of each sentence that suggests the numbered bold vocabulary word. In each group, you may circle more than one letter or none at all.

1. convivial

(a) Whenever we get together with the Simpsons, we have a marvelous time.

(b) Mrs. Rhodes went out of her way to make our stay an enjoyable one.

(c) Jonathan laughingly admitted that his favorite companion was a good book.

2. mogul

(a) Cecil B. DeMille was one of the most powerful studio heads in Hollywood.

(b) The Soviet Union's collapse left the United States as the only superpower.

(c) Ted Turner built a vast entertainment and television news organization.

3. propitious

(a) It seems that Margot will do just about anything to please her mother.

(b) Last month's rainfall of sixteen inches is the highest on record.

(c) The best way to get to Seattle is by way of Chicago and Minneapolis.

4. perspicacity

(a) Joanne could recite her seven times table when she was only six.

(b) No matter how difficult the task, Reggie always refuses to give up.

(c) All the stocks that Nicole picked showed substantial increases in value.

5. anathema

(a) Harriet Beecher Stowe regarded slavery as a loathsome institution.

(b) Robin detests flying and always travels by train.

(c) The topic of Sarita's paper was cooperation between ant species.

6. epigram

(a) Oscar Wilde declared that he could resist anything except temptation.

(b) Experience is the name we give to our mistakes.

(c) President Nixon announced to the entire nation that he was not a crook.

7. nascent

(a) Some historians contend that the American Revolution really began in 1773 with the Boston Tea Party.

(b) Life on earth began nearly four billion years ago.

(c) The company is less than a month old, but sales already exceed projections.

anathema
assuage
avuncular
convivial
eclectic
epigram
expound
intrinsic
inveterate
mogul
munificent
nascent
perspicacious
philistine
propitious

8. **philistine**

   (a) "I know nothing about art, and I have no desire to learn."

   (b) Developers knocked down an architectural gem to build a parking garage.

   (c) Klara was willing to attend the opera as long as she could sleep through it.

9. **munificence**

   (a) The garden is a delight to the senses with its abundance of flowers.

   (b) The government gave billions of dollars in price supports to farmers.

   (c) The generosity of princes made possible the glories of the Renaissance.

10. **avuncular**

   (a) Even though he's only five, Robert is very protective of his baby brother.

   (b) Our neighbor Mr. Staley often took my brother and me to baseball games and even taught us to pitch.

   (c) His pencil-thin moustache and sallow complexion gave him a jaded look.

6E Passage

Read the passage below; then complete the exercise that follows it.

The Dorothy and Herbert Vogel Collection

The National Gallery of Art in Washington, D.C., was a gift to the nation from banking and industry **mogul** Andrew W. Mellon. Although some wealthy people are uncompromising **philistines**, such acts of **munificence** are by no means unheard of among those whose can afford them. Therefore, when visitors to the National Gallery see an exhibition of works from "The Dorothy and Herbert Vogel Collection," they could be excused for thinking that the Vogels are wealthy arts patrons. In fact, nothing could be further from the truth.

Herbert Vogel, a stocky, **avuncular** man with a twinkle in his eye, was a postal clerk in New York City. His wife, Dorothy, was a reference librarian at the Brooklyn Public Library. They married in 1962 and spent their honeymoon in Washington, D.C. Frequent visits to the National Gallery during their stay inspired them to try painting, an effort they soon abandoned. Instead, they became **inveterate** collectors of other people's work. To do so, they lived frugally, using Dorothy's salary to pay their living expenses, while everything Herbert earned was spent acquiring works of art. Though neither came from a wealthy family, they had in common a love of art and considerable **perspicacity** in selecting works from talented artists who were at the beginning of their careers. Many of these artists later became famous, with a corresponding increase in the market value of their work.

New York in the early sixties was an exciting place for artists. Op art, pop art, minimalism, conceptualism— these were just some of the **nascent** movements that would soon take the art world by storm. Painters and sculptors would meet to **expound** their theories and argue with each other at the Cedar Bar in Greenwich Village. Herbert Vogel, who worked irregular hours at the post office, would often take the subway to lower Manhattan to join these **convivial** gatherings. After sitting quietly, listening, and absorbing the ideas being bandied about by the artists, some of whom had yet to sell a single work, he would return home to share his experiences with his wife.

As a result of these encounters, the Vogels became acquainted with a number of artists and began making their first purchases. It was a **propitious** time to start a collection; works that would later sell for tens of thousands of dollars could be bought for mere hundreds or even less. Not that the Vogels would ever disclose what they paid for a particular piece—to put a cash value on any work of art is **anathema** to them. They appreciate their pieces for their **intrinsic** worth, not for what they would bring on the open market. In fact, the Vogels have never tried to cash in on their art collection by selling any of the works acquired over a period of thirty years.

The Vogels' taste in art is **eclectic**; they buy what they love, can afford, and have room for. This last consideration is important, for by 1992, their tiny apartment was crammed with more than two thousand paintings, drawings, and sculptures. It was then that the Vogels decided to give their treasures to the nation. They chose the National Gallery of Art as the recipient of their collection because it does not charge for admission and never sells any of its works of art—a practice common at other museums. Five large vans were needed to move the treasured objects to their new home in the nation's capital. The Vogels **assuaged** whatever sadness they felt at the loss by reflecting on the living space they had gained and on the fact that they will continue to collect, with all future acquisitions going eventually to the National Gallery.

In his play *Lady Windemere's Fan*, Oscar Wilde defines a cynic as someone "who knows the price of everything and the value of nothing." The Vogels reverse this **epigram**, for it can truly be said that, where art is concerned, they know the value of everything and the price of nothing.

Answer each of the following questions in the form of a sentence. If a question does not contain a vocabulary word from this lesson's word list, use one in your answer. Use each word only once.

1. How does the description of Herbert Vogel suggest that he would be a **convivial** companion?

2. How might the Vogels respond to the Roman philosopher Seneca's **epigram** that "life is short but art is long"?

3. How did the Vogels **assuage** their hunger for art?

4. Why were the 1960s a **propitious** time for the Vogels to start collecting?

5. What quality did the Vogels have that compensated for their lack of wealth?

6. How do we know that collecting art became the Vogels' main preoccupation?

anathema
assuage
avuncular
convivial
eclectic
epigram
expound
intrinsic
inveterate
mogul
munificent
nascent
perspicacious
philistine
propitious

7. Why would running a gallery that sold art be an unlikely proposition for the Vogels?

_____

8. Why is the nation fortunate that the Vogels selected the National Gallery of Art as the recipient of their collection?

_____

9. What misconception might someone visiting the Dorothy and Herbert Vogel Collection have about the couple?

_____

10. What, if any, was the focus of the Vogels' art collection?

_____

11. Why would it be inaccurate to describe the Vogels as having a **philistine** attitude?

_____

FUN & FASCINATING FACTS

Until the mid-1700s, when the British established themselves there, northern India was ruled by the Muslim dynasty known as the Moguls. The solider-statesman-poet Babur led their conquest of the region from neighboring Afghanistan in 1526. To the conquered Hindus, a **mogul** was a powerful person; when the British occupied India, the word passed into English with its meaning unchanged.

Note that a **mogul** is also a small, hard mound on a ski slope. This word is derived from an old Scandinavian word *mugi,* "a small hill."

Perspicacious means "clear-sighted; shrewd." It is applied to persons possessing this quality. Don't confuse this word with *perspicuous,* which means "clearly expressed; easy to understand." The latter is generally *not* applied to persons. A report can be perspicuous, and if so, one would not need to be **perspicacious** in order to understand it.

The Philistines were people of Philistia, an ancient region of Palestine, who figure prominently in the Old Testament and never in a favorable light. The giant Goliath, who challenged the Israelites and was slain by David, was a Philistine. It was the Philistines who captured and blinded Samson. When the Bible became readily available following the publication of the 1611 King James version, **philistine** (with a small *p*) entered the language. At first it was a general term for an unworthy person, but over time it acquired its present, more specific meaning.

Lesson 7

Word List
Study the definitions of the words below; then do the exercises for the lesson.

archipelago
är kə pel´ ə gō

n. 1. A large group of islands.
Key West is the southernmost island of the Florida **archipelago** referred to as "the Keys."
2. A body of water containing a large number of islands.
The island of Rhodes is located in the Aegean **archipelago**.

careen
kə rēn´

v. 1. To rush headlong, often with a swerving or lurching motion.
The roller coaster cars **careened** around the bends.
2. To cause to lean or tip to one side (as a ship).
It's thrilling to sail when strong winds **careen** the boat.

cavalier
kav ə lir´

adj. Showing an offhand or carefree disregard; arrogant.
Alexei's **cavalier** attitude toward study may one day catch up with him.

contiguous
kən tig´ yoo əs

adj. Sharing a boundary; being very close or in contact; adjacent.
Properties **contiguous** to the town landfill cost considerably less than those located downtown.

correlate
kôr´ ə lāt

v. To connect related things; to bring things into proper relation with one another.
The study **correlated** the exposure to certain plastics with an increase in cancer cases.
correlation *n.* (kôr ə lā´ shən)
The possible **correlation** between piano playing and mathematical achievement merits further study.

etymology
et ə mäl´ ə jē

n. 1. The history of a word.
The **etymology** of many English words reveals the language's close ties to ancient Latin.
2. The science that studies such histories.
The **etymology** of place names often provides interesting cultural and historical information.

frenetic
fri net´ ik

adj. Wildly excited; frantic.
The **frenetic** buying and selling on the floor of the stock market yesterday left investors wary about today's transactions.

kinetic
ki net´ ik

adj. Relating to motion.
A moving body possesses **kinetic** energy proportional to its speed and mass.

presage
prē sāj´

v. To foretell; to warn or indicate in advance.
Dark clouds **presage** rain.

pulverize
pul´ vər īz

v. 1. To crush or grind into dust or powder.
The limestone was **pulverized** and then used to make cement.
2. To demolish.
The hurricane **pulverized** the beachside cabins until they were unrecognizable.

recondite
rek´ ən dīt

adj. Difficult to understand; abstruse.
The law of primogeniture during the Plantagenet era is one of the **recondite** subjects on which Ms. González is an expert.

repulse
rē puls´

v. 1. To repel; to drive back.
The general was disconcerted when his attack on the enemy position was **repulsed**.
2. To reject in a cool or distant manner.
Catherine **repulsed** his invitation with a curt refusal.
3. To disgust.
The unsavory incident concerning the man and his dogs **repulsed** those who witnessed it.

seismic
sīz´ mik

adj. 1. Caused by or having to do with earthquakes.
Seismic changes in the earth's crust caused the break in the freeway.
2. Having powerful and widespread effects.
The new leadership promises political changes of **seismic** proportions.

undulate
un´ jōō lāt

v. 1. To form or move in waves.
The sea **undulated** beneath the boat, lifting it up and down.
2. To have a wavelike appearance or motion.
The wheat field **undulated** in the wind.
undulation *n.* (un jōō lā´ shən)
Pilar began to feel ill from driving on the steep **undulations** of the country road.

upheaval
up hē´ vəl

n. 1. A radical or violent change.
The Civil Rights movement sparked a time of **upheaval** across the country.
2. A forceful lifting or warping from beneath.
Small **upheavals** in our lawn revealed the subterranean paths of moles.

7A Understanding Meanings

Read the sentences below. If a sentence correctly uses the word in bold, write *C* on the line below it. If a sentence is incorrect, rewrite it so that the vocabulary word in bold is used correctly.

1. To **pulverize** rock is to break it up into chunks.

_____

2. A **recondite** essay is one that is hard to understand.

_____

3. A **cavalier** response is one that is extremely gracious.

_____

4. An **archipelago** is a body of water containing many islands.

_____

5. To **presage** an event is to make preparations for it.

_____

6. An **upheaval** is an instance of forceful lifting from below.

_____

7. **Kinetic** energy is energy that is suppressed.

_____

8. To **repulse** an advance is to push it back with force.

_____

9. **Seismic** waves are those caused by an earthquake.

_____

10. To **correlate** facts is to link them to one another in a systematic manner.

_____

11. To **careen** is to complain in a loud and offensive tone.

_____

12. **Etymology** is the study of insects.

_____

13. **Contiguous** sections are those that can be easily separated.

archipelago
careen   _____
cavalier
contiguous
correlate   14. A **frenetic** movement is one that is hidden from view.
etymology
frenetic   _____
kinetic
presage   15. An **undulation** is a repeated rising and falling.
pulverize
recondite   _____
repulse
seismic
undulate
upheaval

7B Using Words

If the word (or a form of the word) in bold fits a sentence in the group below it, write the word in the blank. If the word does not fit, leave the space empty.

1. **pulverize**

   (a) I used a food processor to _____ the nuts into a smooth paste.

   (b) During World War II, carpet bombing _____ Dresden and its environs.

   (c) Karl's unwillingness to negotiate _____ any chance of an agreement.

2. **undulate**

   (a) A rock dropped into the pond causes the surface of the water to _____ .

   (b) Notice how the rounded hills seem to _____ like ocean waves.

   (c) We saw two snakes _____ across the sand and into the undergrowth.

3. **cavalier**

   (a) The manager brushed aside my complaint in a _____ manner.

   (b) The roof had been repaired in such a _____ fashion that it still leaked badly.

   (c) Deborah's _____ dismissal from the firm after years of service was a shock to younger employees.

4. **repulse**

   (a) An irritated glance was all it took to _____ Arthur's attempt at conversation.

   (b) We _____ the coffee beans to get a very fine grind.

   (c) The film's explicit and gratuitous gore _____ its audience.

5. **careen**

   (a) The pitch _____ past the batter at over 90 mph.

   (b) The crowd cheered as the leading yacht _____ around the marker buoy.

   (c) The truck _____ around the mountain's hairpin turns at an alarming speed.

6. **correlation**

   (a) The _____ between SAT scores and college performance is still unclear.

   (b) The electrical failure was due to a faulty _____ in the circuit.

   (c) There is an unambiguous _____ between cigarette smoking and lung cancer.

7. **presage**

   (a) The quarrels between Shea and Liv do not _____ a healthy friendship for them.

   (b) We decided to _____ the report for discussion at a later time.

   (c) Some people still believe that tea leaves _____ important life events.

8. **contiguous**

(a) Measles is an extremely _____ disease.

(b) The summer cottages are _____ to the beach and less than a mile from the town center.

(c) We spent the entire class discussing the _____ meaning of the novel's ending.

7C Word Study

Choose from the two words provided and use each word only once when filling in the spaces. One space should be left blank.

repulsed/repelled

1. Three times he asked her for a date, and three times she _____ him.

2. To his polite offer to help, she _____ , "Get lost!"

3. The replacement product _____ mosquitoes more effectively than the old one.

assuage/satisfy

4. After cresting at noon, the floodwaters began to _____ .

5. A warm hug is all it took to _____ little Caitlyn's fears.

6. You need two years of math to _____ the requirements for graduation.

acquiesce/comply

7. When two people disagree on a course of action, one of them must _____ .

8. You must _____ with the requirements in order to receive a pass.

9. The speaker started by saying, "I don't expect everyone to _____ with me."

penitent/sorry

10. We were saddened to see the garden was _____ with neglect.

11. The boy who cheated on his exam showed a _____ attitude as he sat before the principal.

12. "I'm _____ to interrupt you," I said and quickly asked my question.

interpose/intervene

13. I was tempted to _____ but decided the argument was none of my business.

14. If you _____ yourself between two people who disagree, you must expect trouble.

15. I was hoping I could _____ myself for the position of general manager.

archipelago
careen
cavalier
contiguous
correlate
etymology
frenetic
kinetic
presage
pulverize
recondite
repulse
seismic
undulate
upheaval

7D Images of Words

Circle the letter of each sentence that suggests the numbered bold vocabulary word. In each group, you may circle more than one letter or none at all.

1. **etymology**

   (a) There are about 850,000 species of insects known to science.

   (b) Chalazae are the thickened strands that attach the egg yolk to the shell.

   (c) Although there have been several explanations, no one is really certain of the origin of the word *ballyhoo.*

2. **frenetic**

   (a) A cry of "Fire!" led to a mad dash for the auditorium's two exits.

   (b) The rush of last-minute holiday shopping in crowded stores exhausts me.

   (c) The crew of the sinking ship scrambled to the rail and plunged into the sea.

3. **recondite**

   (a) Roberta is an expert on the Samurai code of seventeenth-century Japan.

   (b) The English penny black is an extremely rare postage stamp.

   (c) The source of the Nile remained undiscovered by Europeans until 1862.

4. **seismic**

   (a) The dropping of the atomic bombs on Japan had enormous consequences.

   (b) The intensity of an earthquake is measured on the Richter scale.

   (c) The release of stress along a fault in the earth's crust can be catastrophic.

5. **contiguous**

   (a) The road stretched in a straight, unbroken line for as far as we could see.

   (b) The phone rang almost without stopping for four hours this morning.

   (c) The 49th parallel separates Canada and the United States in the west.

6. **archipelago**

   (a) Indonesia, comprising more than 3,000 islands, lies north of Australia.

   (b) The Thousand Islands region lies at the eastern end of Lake Ontario.

   (c) Wisconsin contains over 8,500 lakes, the largest being Lake Winnebago.

7. **undulate**

   (a) The loud tick tock, tick tock of the clock kept Kevin awake until dawn.

   (b) The stock market goes up and down in an irregular manner.

   (c) The road rose and fell rhythmically as it went over a series of small hills.

8. **repulse**

   (a) After reaching the high-water mark, the swollen river finally began to subside.

   (b) The Red Army turned back the advancing German army at Stalingrad.

   (c) It requires an effort to bring the north poles of two magnets together.

9. **kinetic**

   (a) The energy possessed by a large meteorite striking the earth is enormous.

   (b) Calder's mobiles are sculptures that move through defined spaces.

   (c) Esperanza seems jumpy today, as though she's expecting bad news.

10. **upheaval**

   (a) The tremors from the earthquake shook buildings in a ten-mile radius.

   (b) The 1910 Revolution brought enormous social and political changes to Mexico.

   (c) Gloria sat up suddenly, forgetting the cup and saucer balanced on her lap.

7E Passage

Read the passage below; then complete the exercise that follows it.

Tsunami: The Big Wave

Over the centuries, geologists have learned that the earth is anything but a solid ball of rock. They know that the earth's crust is made of massive, interlocking "plates" riding on a molten mantle. These plates move very slowly. When they slide or grind against one another, an earthquake with devastating consequences may be triggered. If such an **upheaval** takes place on the ocean floor, the result can be even more catastrophic, for it may **presage** a tsunami, a series of ocean waves of such force that they can sweep away whole villages and **pulverize** the strongest buildings.

When an undersea section of the earth's crust shifts, it can displace a huge volume of water, releasing an enormous amount of **kinetic** energy. Because this energy is distributed over the entire depth of the water, its effects are not immediately apparent. All that can be seen are slight waves on the surface, even though they are traveling at speeds of over six hundred miles an hour. It is not until these undersea waves reach shallower waters that they unleash their awesome power. The energy that may have been diffused over a depth of several miles is now concentrated in water just hundreds of feet deep and getting shallower. A wave's velocity decreases, but its compressed energy forces it to grow in size. What might have begun several thousand miles away as a slight surface **undulation** two or three feet high becomes a wall of water thirty, sixty, even a hundred feet high which smashes everything in its path.

The coastal regions most in danger from tsunamis are those **contiguous** to the Pacific Ocean, where undersea geological events are more frequent. A tsunami powerful enough to cause serious damage occurs in the Pacific about every ten to fifteen years. Japan is especially prone to tsunamis since an area of intense **seismic** activity lies close to its eastern shore. The **etymology** of the name *tsunami* reflects Japan's familiarity with this terrifying phenomenon; it comes from two Japanese words, *tsu* (harbor) and *nami* (wave). Because the Japanese tsunamis have such a short distance to travel, coastal dwellers receive almost no warning of their onslaught. In the most vulnerable areas tall seawalls have been built to **repulse** the tsunami, but even a fifty-foot wall is of little value against a sixty- or hundred-foot wall of water.

The Hawaiian **archipelago**, located in the mid-Pacific and with no large land masses close by, is also particularly vulnerable to tsunamis. In 1946, an earthquake measuring 7.8 on the Richter

archipelago
careen
cavalier
contiguous
correlate
etymology
frenetic
kinetic
presage
pulverize
recondite
repulse
seismic
undulate
upheaval

scale and centered near Alaska's Aleutian Islands set off a tsunami, estimated to be over one hundred feet high when it reached the Alaskan coast. Traveling at 490 miles per hour, it struck Hawaii about five hours later. Waves fifty feet high flooded the coast, killing 173 people.

As a result of the 1946 disaster, the United States government established the Pacific Tsunami Warning Center, located just outside Honolulu. There, seismologists (scientists who study earthquakes) practice the **recondite** science of tsunami prediction by monitoring plate activity over a wide area of the Pacific. Prolonged quiet spells are punctuated by periods of **frenetic** action when the needles on sensing instruments start jumping, indicating an earthquake. The seismologists quickly **correlate** all the data they are receiving to pinpoint the location of the earthquake and estimate the likelihood of a tsunami striking, as well as its possible magnitude.

On the morning of December 26, 2004, a powerful earthquake, measuring 9.0 on the Richter scale, struck beneath the sea off the west coast of Sumatra, Indonesia. The earthquake—the fourth largest since 1900—sent a huge wall of water **careening** across the Indian Ocean. Waves over 100 feet high crashed without warning on the shores of several South Asian countries. The hardest hit were Indonesia, Sri Lanka, India, and Thailand. All told, more than 280,000 people lost their lives in this disaster. Millions more were among the missing and injured. The force of the tsunami was so intense that entire coastal villages and resorts were washed away.

Afterwards, many wondered why there was no warning that the giant wave was coming. While countries of the Pacific Rim have a system that gives them from three to fourteen hours' warning of a tsunami, there is no such system in effect in the Indian Ocean countries. A mixture of circumstances such as poverty and remoteness of the various islands—not a **cavalier** attitude toward these giant waves—is most likely responsible for this situation. Anyone who has witnessed a tsunami understands the importance of providing this warning and will never forget this most fearsome of natural disasters.

Answer each of the following questions in the form of a sentence. If a question does not contain a vocabulary word from this lesson's word list, use one in your answer. Use each word only once.

1. Explain the **etymology** of *tsunami*.

2. What are two things that Alaska, California, and Japan have in common?

3. Why are many of the **archipelagoes** located in the Pacific so vulnerable to tsunamis?

4. What can be the consequence of a shift by one of the plates in the earth's crust?

5. How powerful is a large tsunami?

6. Why might a person at sea not recognize a tsunami in its early stages?

7. Why do you think the science of predicting tsunamis is described as **recondite**?

8. Why would people who take a **cavalier** attitude toward a tsunami alert be a problem for public safety officials?

9. What **presages** an earthquake to seismologists?

10. Why can seawalls offer only partial protection against tsunamis?

FUN & FASCINATING FACTS

Career as a verb means "to move at high speed." **Careen** was originally a sailing term meaning "to tilt to one side when turning." Perhaps confusion between these two terms led to *career* taking on its present primary meaning, which can be thought of as a combination of the two original terms. *Career* is now infrequently used except in its well-known role as a noun.

The English Civil War (1642–48) was fought between the Cavaliers, followers of King Charles I, and the Roundheads, supporters of parliamentary government, so called for their closely cropped hair. The king's supporters believed that he ruled by divine right and were disdainful of those who believed otherwise. The Royalists lost the war and Charles lost his head; *cavalier*, without the capital *c* but with the dismissive Royalist attitude, entered the language.

Lesson 8

Word List

Study the definitions of the words below; then do the exercises for the lesson.

betrothed
bē trōthd´

adj. Engaged to be married.
The **betrothed** couple exchanged gifts to mark their engagement.
n. A person to whom one is engaged to be married.
Charles gave his **betrothed** an emerald engagement ring.

blasphemy
blas´ fə mē

n. An act or statement that shows disrespect or irreverence toward something considered sacred.
Michele did not observe the holy days and was thus accused of **blasphemy**.

cadence
kād´ ns

n. 1. A rhythm marked by a regular beat.
The crowd thrilled to the **cadence** of marching feet as the parade passed by.
2. The rising and falling of the voice in human speech.
I could tell by the **cadence** of the stranger's speech that he was extremely agitated.

canon
kan´ ən

n. 1. A rule or principle that provides the norm for judgment.
Those who would not conform to the **canons** of polite society became social outcasts.
2. The works of a writer accepted as authentic.
The recent discovery of an unpublished short story adds to the Eudora Welty **canon**.

denouement
dā noō mä´

(A French word now part of our vocabulary.) *n.* 1. The outcome of a series of events.
The sudden collapse of the Soviet Union provided an unexpected **denouement** to the Cold War.
2. The final resolution following the climax of the plot of a work of drama or fiction.
The death of the king provides a fitting **denouement** to Shakespeare's *Richard III*.

edict
ē´ dikt

n. A statement or command having the force of law.
The czar's **edict** banning public demonstrations was ignored by the Russian people.

enamor
en am´ ər

(Usually used with *of* or *with*) *v.* To inspire with love; to captivate.
The director was especially **enamored** of a fine bronze statue by Cellini.

insensate
in sen´ sāt

adj. 1. Lacking sensation or awareness.
When the rescue team reached the skier trapped in the snow, they found her alive, but **insensate**, with no awareness of her surroundings.
2. Lacking sense or ability to reason.
The artist captures the **insensate** fury of a storm at sea.
3. Brutal; lacking feeling.
Because he had no empathy for the feelings of other people, he committed **insensate** acts of violence.

renegade
ren´ ə gād

n. 1. A person who deserts one group or cause for another; a traitor.
Winston Churchill was regarded as a **renegade** for deserting the Conservative party to join the Liberals.
2. A person who rejects lawful behavior.
Some people considered Margaret Sanger a **renegade** because of her attempts to provide family planning information to women, in an age when such activity was illegal.

soliloquy sə lil′ ə kwē	*n.* A speech in which a character's thoughts are given verbal expression. Hamlet's most famous **soliloquy** begins, "To be or not to be."
stricture strik′ chər	(Usually plural) *n.* 1. A strong criticism. The president, unable to ignore the **strictures** of the press, was forced to issue an apology for his remarks. 2. Anything that restricts or limits. The treaty removes many of the **strictures** hampering free trade between the two countries.
triumvirate trī um′ vər ət	*n.* A group of three, especially one possessing great power or eminence. After displacing the other two members of the **triumvirate**, the general ruled the country as a dictator.
usurp yo͞o sʉrp′	*v.* To seize and hold power or authority in an illegal or unjust manner. When the wealthy landowners tried to **usurp** power from the queen, she outmaneuvered them.
vestment vest′ mənt	(Often plural) *n.* An outer garment, especially one indicating a role, rank, or office. The exquisite **vestments** worn by an eighteenth-century empress are on display in the museum.
votary vōt′ ə rē	*n.* A person who is devoted to a cause or organization, especially one of a religious nature. The **votaries** of Demeter gathered at Eleusis for special ceremonies honoring the goddess.

8A Understanding Meanings

Read the sentences below. If a sentence correctly uses the word in bold, write *C* on the line below it. If a sentence is incorrect, rewrite it so that the vocabulary word in bold is used correctly.

1. **Cadence** is the fluctuation of a person's speaking voice.

_____

2. To be **enamored** of someone is to be envious of that person.

betrothed
blasphemy
cadence
canon
denouement
edict
enamor
insensate
renegade
soliloquy
stricture
triumvirate
usurp
vestment
votary

_____

3. **Strictures** are restrictions placed on an activity.

_____

4. To become **insensate** is to lose consciousness.

_____

5. A play's **denouement** is the message it is intended to carry.

_____

6. To be **betrothed** is to be sworn in as a witness in court.

7. A **triumvirate** is a decisive victory over one's enemies.

8. A **renegade** is one who refuses to take a firm stand on an issue.

9. To **usurp** authority is to take it unrightfully.

10. **Vestments** are items of clothing with special significance.

11. An **edict** is a decree issued by a person in authority.

12. To commit **blasphemy** is to speak reverently of one's god.

13. A **soliloquy** is an exchange of dialog between characters.

14. A **canon** is a weapon of war.

15. A **votary** is an enthusiastic and faithful follower.

8B Using Words

If the word (or a form of the word) in bold fits in a sentence in the group below it, write the word in the blank. If the word does not fit, leave the space empty.

1. **cadence**

   (a) The powerful _____ of the poet's voice gripped the audience.

   (b) We closed the window near the road to shut out the traffic's _____ .

   (c) The visitor spoke with a visitor _____ that I had difficulty understanding.

2. **vestment**

   (a) Ms. Morrison and the other honorees each wore special _____ for the recognition ceremony.

   (b) Salt, pepper, and other _____ were placed on every table.

   (c) My parents always said that buying this house when they did was a very good _____ .

3. **stricture**

   (a) Metal fatigue had caused tiny _____ in the wing panels.

   (b) The _____ of this bridge requires repair immediately.

   (c) Unlike some of my friends, I welcome the _____ of life at this summer camp.

4. **usurp**

   (a) If I got up to get something in the kitchen, my dog, Sly, would _____ my spot on the sofa.

   (b) Caesar's attempt to _____ power in Rome led to his downfall.

   (c) Someone _____ my purse while I was away from my desk.

5. **votary**

   (a) As we entered the ancient cathedral, the only light came from a cluster of _____ burning on a low table.

   (b) A large number of people showed up at the _____ on election day.

   (c) Those who had once been the senator's _____ now turned on her.

6. **edict**

   (a) The governor's _____ banned oil tankers from entering the bay.

   (b) The _____ reminded the students to check their schedules.

   (c) The most important _____ of a doctor is to do no harm.

7. **soliloquy**

   (a) I fell into a deep _____ during which my mind was a complete blank.

   (b) To say that might makes right is to utter a _____ .

   (c) I left the pair alone, not wishing to interrupt their _____ .

betrothed
blasphemy
cadence
canon
denouement
edict
enamor
insensate
renegade
soliloquy
stricture
triumvirate
usurp
vestment
votary

8C Word Study

Fill in the missing word in each of the sentences below. Then write a brief definition of the word. The number in parentheses gives the lesson from which the word
is taken.

1. The Latin prefix *ex-* means "out." It combines with the Latin *plicare* (to fold)

   to form the English _____ (5), meaning

   _____ .

2. The prefix *tri-* means "three." It combines with the Greek *virum* (of men)

   to form the English word _____ (8), meaning

   _____ .

3. The prefix *con-* means "with." It combines with the Latin *veer* (to live)

   to form the English word _____ (6), meaning

   _____ .

4. The Latin words *munus* (gift) and *facere* (to make) combine to

   form the English word _____ (6), meaning

   _____ .

5. The Latin word *nasci* (to be born) forms the English word _____ (6),

   meaning _____ .

6. The prefix *per-* means "through." It combines with the Latin *specare* (to look)

   to form the English word _____ (6), meaning

   _____ .

7. The Greek words *archi* (ancient) and *pelago* (sea) combine to

   form the English word _____ (7), meaning

   _____ .

8. The prefix *con-* means "together." It combines with the Latin *tangere* (to touch)

   to form the English word _____ (7), meaning

   _____ .

9. The Latin words *solus* (alone) and *loqui* (to speak) combine to

   form the English word _____ (8), meaning

   _____ .

10. The Greek words *etumos* (true) and *logos* (word) combine to

form the English word _____ (7), meaning

_____ .

8D Images of Words

Circle the letter of each sentence that suggests the numbered bold vocabulary word. In each group, you may circle more than one letter or none at all.

1. **vestments**

   (a) Bonnie checks the value of her stocks every day.

   (b) It is very difficult for a confirmed smoker to quit.

   (c) In some parts of the world, people wear white to show mourning.

2. **cadence**

   (a) The lawyer wanted us to read all of the terms of the agreement before we signed.

   (b) The metronome helps the pianist to maintain a strict tempo.

   (c) Our cottage was close enough to the ocean for us to awake each morning to the sound of the waves.

3. **triumvirate**

   (a) The Three Stooges are my favorite comedy team of all time.

   (b) Marc Antony, Octavian, and Marcus Lepidus ruled Rome together.

   (c) Our team was among the top three in the state basketball rankings.

4. **renegade**

   (a) Bloom's latest novel is a complete departure from her previous books.

   (b) Benedict Arnold switched sides during the Revolutionary War.

   (c) The insurance company raised Cho's rates after his third accident.

5. **blasphemy**

   (a) Muslims believe that speaking contemptuously of Muhammad is irreverent.

   (b) Many societies have laws against acting disrespectfully toward deities.

   (c) Catalina seemed indifferent to the fact that she had won a thousand dollars.

6. **enamor**

   (a) I couldn't decide between the egg salad and the toasted cheese.

   (b) Did you notice that couple holding hands at the table in back?

   (c) Elm is a difficult wood to work with.

7. **soliloquy**

   (a) In his half-awake state he felt he was floating.

   (b) "Half a loaf is better than no bread."

   (c) Beth had to settle for no more than an honorable mention.

betrothed
blasphemy
cadence
canon
denouement
edict
enamor
insensate
renegade
soliloquy
stricture
triumvirate
usurp
vestment
votary

8. **canon**

    (a) I have a complete set of the works of Virginia Woolf.

    (b) Be careful what you wish for; you might get it.

    (c) You must follow the rules of scientific experimentation to achieve acceptable results.

9. **stricture**

    (a) The building survived the earthquake intact.

    (b) The chairman failed to turn the company around despite his promise.

    (c) With my leg in a cast I found it impossible to drive a car.

10. **denouement**

    (a) Sally informed us that she would never eat meat again.

    (b) The final act of the play reveals that Jenkins and Boxer are one and the same person.

    (c) The impeachment attempt failed in the Senate by one vote.

8E Passage

Read the passage below; then complete the exercise that follows it.

The Gift of Tragedy

What do movies, TV sitcoms, stage plays, and grand opera all have in common? All four can trace their origin back twenty-five centuries to the inventiveness of a Greek nobleman named Aeschylus, who lived from c. 525 to c. 456 B.C. He is one of the **triumvirate** of Greek writers, together with Sophocles and Euripides, who refined tragedy as a literary form and helped make Athens the cradle of Western civilization in the fifth century B.C.

As a young man living in Athens, Aeschylus was among the thousands of **votaries** of Dionysus who attended the great festivals honoring the god. Citizens competed to have their work performed at these events, which combined music, dance, and choral recitations. A feature of these performances was an interlude in which the leader of the chorus and an actor known as the "answerer" delivered a series of **soliloquies** to the audience.

In 499 B.C., Aeschylus competed in this event, as he would continue to do for the next forty years. His great accomplishment was to refuse to be bound by the **strictures** of the past. He introduced a second actor so that the two could address each other in true stage dialogue in imitation of an action. In this sense, Aeschylus can be said to have invented character and plot, the twin essentials of drama as we know it today. In addition, he broadened his subject matter to include themes drawn from history and ancient myth. Most notably, he elevated the language of the drama; his stately **cadences**, whether spoken or sung, gave it a nobility appropriate to his tragic themes. The Aeschylean **canon** consists of about ninety plays, of which only seven have survived whole; we know of the remainder only through fragments or contemporary references.

The characters in Aeschylus' plays are not ones audience members would be likely to identify with easily. In *Prometheus*, for example, with one minor exception, they are all deities. Prometheus is regarded as a **renegade** by the other gods for stealing the secret of fire from them and giving it to humans. The action of the play is minimal, consisting of a sequence of visitors to Prometheus, who is chained to a rock as punishment for his misdeed.

The second great playwright of this era, Sophocles (c. 496–406 B.C.), wrote more than one hundred plays, of which only seven survive. He is the probable creator of the innovation of bringing in a third actor, thereby increasing the scope of the drama; he is also believed to have introduced painted scenery, giving his plays a more realistic touch. His characters are on an all-too-human scale, and audiences from ancient times to the present have readily identified with them.

Antigone, in the play of the same name, is one of the great Sophoclean tragic heroines. Her brother Polyneices has been killed in a violent but unsuccessful attempt to **usurp** the throne of Creon, ruler of Thebes. Creon, in an affront to divine law, denies him proper burial. When Antigone defies his **edict** by performing the burial ceremonies over the body, he orders her put to death even though she is **betrothed** to his son Haemon. In a fit of rage, Haemon berates his father, but Creon is adamant. Warned by the blind prophet Tiresias that he has committed **blasphemy** against the gods, Creon, after giving himself time to reflect, has a change of heart, but too late: Antigone has hanged herself. In despair, Haemon also commits suicide, as does Creon's wife, Eurydice. Creon, whose offense was to keep a corpse among the living, himself becomes "a living corpse," as he acknowledges in the final moments of the play.

Sophocles said of his younger rival Euripides (c. 480–406 B.C.) that while he, Sophocles, represented people as they ought to be, Euripides represented them as they are. Nineteen of Euripides' ninety-two plays have survived, and they contain a whole gallery of strong-willed characters whose violent passions are the driving force leading to the drama's tragic **denouement**. His chief characters, many of them women, are drawn with such complexity that the audience's sympathies are often divided or shift in the course of the play. Medea, in the play of that name, first arouses our pity as a woman of powerful emotions whose husband, Jason, brings her to a land where she feels like a stranger. When he becomes **enamored** of another woman, her **insensate** rage leads her to murder their two children. In various modern translations, the play continues to enjoy widespread popularity today, almost twenty-five hundred years after it was written.

Euripides died in 406 B.C. In tribute to his friend and rival of over fifty years, the ninety-year-old Sophocles modified the **vestments** of the performers in his current production as a show of mourning. A few months later, Sophocles too was dead, and the golden age of Greek tragedy came to an end.

Answer each of the following questions in the form of a sentence. If a question does not contain a vocabulary word from this lesson's word list, use one in your answer. Use each word only once.

1. Why would Creon have regarded Polyneices as a **renegade**?

2. What **canon** of the gods did Creon violate?

3. How does Creon respond when Haemon berates him?

4. What happens to Haemon's **betrothed**?

5. Would it be accurate to say that Prometheus was punished for **blasphemy**? Explain your answer.

betrothed
blasphemy
cadence
canon
denouement
edict
enamor
insensate
renegade
soliloquy
stricture
triumvirate
usurp
vestment
votary

6. Why would it be inaccurate to describe Antigone as a **votary** of Creon?

7. Describe the **denouement** of *Medea*.

8. Upon the death of Euripides, what gesture did Sophocles make to show him respect?

9. What **strictures** of Greek drama did Sophocles ignore?

10. What details in the passage suggest that Euripides' characters did not speak in stately or noble **cadences**?

11. In what way were the plays of Euripides different from the early dramatic works performed at the festivals honoring Dionysus?

12. Why do you think it is appropriate to describe Aeschylus, Sophocles, and Euripides as the **triumvirate** of Greek drama?

FUN & FASCINATING FACTS

A couple who become **betrothed** are promising to be true to each other, as the word itself suggests. It is formed from the Old English word *treowth*, meaning "truth."

A play's **denouement** is the part at the end where the plot finally unravels. The word's French pronunciation indicates from which language it entered English, but it can be traced back to the Latin *nodus*, "a knot." This became the French *nouer*, "to tie," as well as its opposite *de(s)nouer*, "to untie or unravel." As a noun it became a literary term in both French and English.

Review for Lessons 5–8

Hidden Message In the boxes provided, write the words from Lessons 5 through 8 that are missing in each of the sentences below. The number following each sentence gives the word list from which the missing word is taken. When the exercise is finished, the shaded boxes will spell out a quotation from the Nobel Prize–winning scientist Marie Curie.

1. Meeta was called a(n) _____ for betraying the cause. (8)

2. If he did _____ to be the manager, then he lied. (5)

3. Code breaking is an extremely _____ science. (5)

4. The riots created a major _____ in the city. (7)

5. I beg you to do nothing to _____ your good name. (5)

6. The _____ pace of the group was too much for me. (7)

7. Real estate _____ Marjorie Ortega is worth billions. (6)

8. Must you _____ to their every demand? (5)

9. Hector seemed truly _____ for his misdeeds. (5)

10. Ms. Sung was quite _____ in the instructions she left. (5)

11. I managed to _____ two tickets to the concert. (5)

12. A(n) _____ of wheat kept the price low. (5)

13. I watched the cars _____ around the track. (7)

14. A(n) _____ party was part of the festivities. (6)

15. The _____ movement was nipped in the bud. (6)

16. A(n) _____ gambler puts everything at risk. (6)

17. Al and Meg were _____ in a candlelit ceremony. (8)

18. Her close relationship with the embezzler casts doubt on _____ . (5)

19. I used a large hammer to _____ the rocks. (7)

20. At the time, ten dollars seemed a _____ sum. (6)

21. After I _____ the data, I'll give my report. (7)

22. Felipe's messy room showed his _____ attitude toward cleanliness. (7)

23. The payments will soon _____ if left untouched. (5)

24. Her _____ taste excluded no type of music. (6)

25. We clapped our hands to the _____ of the music. (8)

26. Alberta and Saskatchewan are _____ provinces. (7)

27. A large meteorite has tremendous _____ energy. (7)

28. A(n) _____ sees little value in the finer things. (6)

29. You commit _____ when you mock the name of their god. (8)

30. Quantum physics is a most _____ science. (7)

31. His _____ smile reminds me of my Uncle Bob. (6)

32. The actress delivered the _____ in a firm voice. (8)

33. He was an admitted _____ of the cult leader. (8)

34. Now is the most _____ time for us to act. (6)

35. He will _____ at length on the value of art. (6)

36. The slight _____ disturbance rattled a few windows. (7)

37. Kind words could not _____ the pain he felt. (6)

38. _____ rage left her indifferent to reason. (8)

39. The tsar's _____ banned all foreign travel. (8)

40. These wooly caterpillars _____ a cold winter. (7)

41. A good _____ should be wise, witty, and brief. (6)

42. The claim that he tried to _____ power is false. (8)

43. Work on the holy days was _____ to some church members. (6)

44. The Balzac _____ includes novels and short stories. (8)

45. Word origins appeal to a student of _____ . (7)

46. See how the marsh reeds _____ in the breeze. (7)

Lesson 9

Word List
Study the definitions of the words below; then do the exercises for the lesson.

advent
ad´ vent
n. A coming or arrival.
With the **advent** of the suburban shopping mall, many small shops downtown closed their doors.

blasé
blä zā´
(A French word now part of our vocabulary.) *adj.* Indifferent to what others might find pleasurable or exciting because of excessive indulgence or enjoyment; unconcerned.
Ethel was **blasé** about winning a Caribbean vacation because she had already visited Aruba several times.

bravado
brə vä´ dō
n. An ostentatious display of bravery; defiant or swaggering behavior.
Frank's latest act of **bravado** was competing in the bungee jump at the Extreme Games.

disparate
dis´ pə rət
adj. 1. Containing or made up of fundamentally different and often incongruous elements.
Shoshana's resumé showed that she had held **disparate** jobs, from editor to magician to sailor.
2. Showing a marked difference or inequality.
Income distribution in the United States has become increasingly **disparate** since the 1980s.
disparity *n.* (di spar´ ə tē)
There is a great **disparity** between Ping's grand ambitions and her modest achievements.

domicile
däm´ ə sīl
n. One's house or place of residence.
The governor's **domicile** was an imposing edifice.

fabricate
fab´ ri kāt
n. 1. To make by putting parts together; to construct.
The canoes are **fabricated** from sheet aluminum.
2. To invent in order to deceive.
An aggrieved former employee **fabricated** the story that the company was going bankrupt.
fabrication *n.*
The rumor that this Mayan artifact is a fake is nothing but a **fabrication**.

itinerant
ī tin´ ər ənt
adj. Traveling from place to place.
The **itinerant** theater group received warm welcomes in the many small towns where it performed.
n. One who goes from place to place.
For three months last year, I was an **itinerant** in India, traveling from one village to another.

lilliputian
li lə pyoo´ shən
adj. Extremely small or appearing to be so.
As we walked around the model village, we towered over the **lilliputian** houses.

phobia
fō´ bē ə
n. A strong, irrational fear.
Although terrified of snakes, I overcame my **phobia** by forcing myself to handle them.

proclivity
prō kli´ və tē
n. A strong inclination towards something.
A **proclivity** for telling stories accounts for Laslo's reputation as a raconteur.

projectile
prə jek´ tīl
n. An object impelled with force or self-propelled through the air.
The strange **projectile** captured on film turned out to be a hubcap tossed in front of the camera.

queasy
kwē´ zē

adj. 1. Causing nausea or tending to be nauseous.
The pitching and rolling of the boat made some passengers **queasy**.
2. Causing or experiencing uneasiness; squeamish.
I felt **queasy** about saying I didn't know where you were when, in fact, I did.

reciprocate
rē sip´ rə kāt

v. To exchange in kind; to repay.
I thanked them for inviting me and promised to **reciprocate** by making them dinner in the near future.
reciprocal *adj.*
This was not a case of unrequited love, but one in which affection was **reciprocal**.
reciprocity *n.* (res ə präs´ ə tē)
This agreement will establish **reciprocity** in cultural exchanges between the two countries.

relegate
rel´ ə gāt

v. 1. To put out of sight or mind; demote.
Wade was mortified when he was **relegated** to a minor league team.
2. To assign for a decision or further action.
These matters have been **relegated** to the subcommittee for additional study.

vertigo
vʉr´ ti gō

n. Dizziness or a tilting, spinning sensation.
Children sometimes induce **vertigo** by spinning around and then immediately trying to walk.

9A Understanding Meanings

Read the sentences below. If a sentence correctly uses the word in bold, write *C* on the line below it. If a sentence is incorrect, rewrite it so that the vocabulary word in bold is used correctly.

1. To feel **queasy** is to have an upset stomach.

_____

2. A **phobia** is a trivial objection.

_____

3. A **reciprocal** agreement is one that benefits both parties.

_____

4. To **fabricate** a story is to piece it together from various sources.

_____

5. A **proclivity** for something is the demonstrated ability to do it.

_____

advent
blasé
bravado
disparate
domicile
fabricate
itinerant
lilliputian
phobia
proclivity
projectile
queasy
reciprocate
relegate
vertigo

6. **Itinerant** musicians are those who will work without emoluments.

7. The **advent** of something is the subtle suggestion of it.

8. A **disparity** is a marked difference between two things being compared.

9. To **relegate** a matter is to hand it over to be acted upon.

10. A **projectile** is an estimate of future income or expenditure.

11. **Bravado** is an ostentatious display of courage.

12. A person who is **blasé** is hard to impress.

13. A **domicile** is a person's place of employment.

14. **Vertigo** is being in an upright position.

15. **Lilliputian** figures appear to be very small.

9B Using Words

If the word (or a form of the word) in bold fits in a sentence in the group below it, write the word in the blank. If the word does not fit, leave the space empty.

1. proclivity

(a) Atsuko's _____ for music developed at an early age.

(b) Children should not be forced into activities for which they show no _____ .

(c) The car rolled down the _____ and came to a stop at a rise in the road.

2. reciprocate

(a) If you'll take care of my dog next week, I'll be glad to _____ .

(b) Kay and I agreed to _____ jobs for a week to see what it was like.

(c) Karim gets upset if you fail to _____ when he pays you a compliment.

3. lilliputian

(a) When I looked through the wrong end of the binoculars, my family appeared _____ .

(b) From 10,000 feet, we looked down on the _____ landscape.

(c) Leah was entranced by the _____ garments in the closets of the doll house.

4. advent

(a) The _____ of television gave advertisers a powerful marketing tool.

(b) The _____ of the Cold War followed the end of World War II.

(c) The entire journey from _____ to end took almost eight months.

5. fabricate

(a) The local machine shop can _____ the parts out of metal strips.

(b) The temptation to _____ data to fit one's theory must be resisted.

(c) The children asked me to help them _____ a snowman.

6. relegate

(a) Not every _____ to the convention is committed to a particular candidate.

(b) We can safely _____ these matters to the mayor's press secretary.

(c) We must _____ these hard-to-sell books to the half-price shelves.

7. queasy

(a) Jen felt _____ about admitting that the prank had been her idea.

(b) Just the thought of getting on the roller coaster made me _____ .

(c) Eating an entire pizza turned out to be no _____ task.

advent
blasé
bravado
disparate
domicile
fabricate
itinerant
lilliputian
phobia
proclivity
projectile
queasy
reciprocate
relegate
vertigo

8. **projectile**

   (a) The _____ fired from the cannon had a range of two miles.

   (b) Beatriz was the manager of the two-year _____ that involved people from five different countries.

   (c) The _____ hovered in the air just inches above the ground.

9C Word Study

A base word can change its part of speech by changing or dropping its suffix or by adding a suffix. Change each of the <u>nouns</u> below into an <u>adjective</u> by changing or dropping the suffix or by adding the correct suffix. Write the word in the space provided. Both forms of all of the words in this exercise are from this lesson or an earlier one.

<u>Noun</u>	<u>Adjective</u>
1. autonomy	_____
2. increment	_____
3. periphery	_____
4. opulence	_____
5. efficacy	_____

Change each of the <u>verbs</u> below into a <u>noun</u> by changing or dropping the suffix or by adding the correct suffix. Write the word in the space provided.

<u>Verb</u>	<u>Noun</u>
6. undulate	_____
7. reciprocate	_____
8. fabricate	_____
9. acquiesce	_____
10. correlate	_____

Change each of the <u>adjectives</u> below into a <u>noun</u> by changing or dropping the suffix or by adding the correct suffix. Write the word in the space provided.

<u>Adjective</u>	<u>Noun</u>
11. penitent	_____
12. reciprocal	_____
13. perspicacious	_____
14. munificent	_____
15. disparate	_____

9D Images of Words

Circle the letter of each sentence that suggests the numbered bold vocabulary word. In each group, you may circle more than one letter or none at all.

1. **itinerant**

   (a) For two months, the best-selling author traveled the country promoting his latest book.

   (b) A letter mailed in New York can now be delivered in Seattle the next day.

   (c) The band estimated it had played in over a hundred towns in one year.

2. **proclivity**

   (a) The stock market declined again yesterday for the fourth straight day.

   (b) Mozart was composing music and performing in public at the age of five.

   (c) The path down to the lake was so steep I almost stumbled several times.

3. **reciprocity**

   (a) The United States will ease trade restrictions if China agrees to respect human rights.

   (b) The job pays four hundred dollars for a forty-hour work week.

   (c) Terry babysits for Sidney while Sidney does Terry's grocery shopping.

4. **domicile**

   (a) Armando works at the Powers Building in midtown Manhattan.

   (b) She lives at 17 Elm Street, on the corner of Elm and Madison.

   (c) My new post office box number is 223.

5. **fabrication**

   (a) Despite what he told you, Jan did not appear in several Hollywood movies.

   (b) The house was constructed in eight hours from sections trucked to the site.

   (c) Hugo has been taking medication to control irregular contractions of his heart.

6. **blasé**

   (a) On her return from India, Marcella pronounced the Taj Mahal "boring."

   (b) The reviewer described Anders's latest novel as "unreadable."

   (c) Carson's third trip aboard the space shuttle was "strictly routine."

7. **phobia**

   (a) Carol refuses to eat meat because she opposes the killing of animals.

   (b) When Tarik saw the spider, he fled from the room in a panic.

   (c) Mrs. Hobbs is frequently worried about her son's driving.

advent
blasé
bravado
disparate
domicile
fabricate
itinerant
lilliputian
phobia
proclivity
projectile
queasy
reciprocate
relegate
vertigo

8. **disparity**

   (a) After the meeting I talked with one of my old friends from high school.

   (b) Joey complained that his sister got a much bigger piece of pie than he did.

   (c) The CEO earns a hundred times more than do entry-level workers.

9. **bravado**

   (a) Unarmed youths ran up to the soldiers and shouted insults at them.

   (b) Daring the others to follow her, Juanita jumped thirty feet into the river.

   (c) The child underwent a dozen serious operations without once complaining.

10. **vertigo**

   (a) Jerome cannot eat spicy food because it makes him nauseated.

   (b) Beth clung to my arm for support when she felt the room spin around her.

   (c) Looking down from the tower made me dizzy, and I was afraid I'd fall.

9E Passage

Read the passage below; then complete the exercise that follows it.

Reaching the Heights

Fear of heights is a common **phobia**. In mild cases, this fear amounts to no more than the **queasy** feeling many people get when looking down from a tall building at the **lilliputian** people walking far below. In extreme cases, it can trigger an acute attack of **vertigo**. Curiously, this fear tends to lessen when people are no longer in contact with the ground, even if they are very high up. Think of how **blasé** most people are when called to board an airliner.

Because few people want to risk their lives working hundreds of feet in the air on tall structures, builders pay high wages to those who are able and willing to do so. That was the case when the Dominion Bridge Steel Company proposed building a bridge over the Saint Lawrence River, near Quebec City, in the 1880s. One end of the bridge was to be on Mohawk land; tribal leaders gave the company permission to build there provided that the company **reciprocate** by agreeing to hire a certain number of Mohawks to work on the project. The new workers, however, had no experience with construction and were **relegated** to positions as unskilled laborers.

As the bridge progressed, skilled riveters perched precariously above the river were astonished to see these laborers making their way nonchalantly along high, narrow girders (beams) to watch them at their work. Some riveters attributed the Mohawks' actions to **bravado**; others believed that they simply felt no fear of heights.

One of the project managers, seeing their curiosity about the project, wondered if the Mohawks would be interested in learning riveting and other skilled jobs. Given the **disparity** in the hourly wages for laborers and the skilled ironworkers, the Mohawks readily said yes. Before long, several Mohawk riveting crews were at work. The first member would heat the rivets in a bucket of hot coals resting on a plank. When one was red-hot, he would remove it with a pair of tongs and toss the glowing **projectile** to the second crew member, who caught it in a bucket and then placed it in a hole through two steel beams. The third member, using a tool called a dollar bar, held it in place, while the fourth flattened the end with a rivet gun. In this way, the steel girders were fastened together. When the bridge was completed, the Native American crews moved on to other projects in Canada. They were soon joined by other Mohawks who shared their **proclivity** for moving nimbly on narrow walkways far above the ground.

The twenty-one-story Flatiron Building, completed in 1902, marked the **advent** of the Manhattan skyscraper-building boom, which reached its peak in the 1920s. Tall buildings sprouted like mushrooms, creating an enormous demand for skilled ironworkers, which Mohawk crews traveled south to satisfy. They helped to **fabricate** the steel skeleton of the 1,250-foot Empire State Building in 1930, for many years the tallest building on earth, and twenty years later helped erect a 204-foot television antenna on top of it.

The first Mohawks began arriving in New York in the early 1920s and found **domiciles** in Brooklyn. Previously forced to live as **itinerant** workers, they now led settled lives with their families and had only to travel across the East River by subway to reach the Manhattan work sites. During the 1960s and 1970s when there were again many construction jobs in New York, the Mohawk community grew to some 1,000 people. The Cuyler Presbyterian Church offered services conducted in Mohawk, and local restaurants sometimes served authentic Mohawk dishes. The section around Brooklyn's Pacific Street became another tiny piece in the ethnic mosaic that makes up New York. When the building boom finally declined in the last decades of the century, many families returned to their former homes in Canada and northern New York.

Answer each of the following questions in the form of a sentence. If a question does not contain a vocabulary word from this lesson's word list, use one in your answer. Use each word only once.

1. Why would someone with a fear of heights be unlikely to be **blasé** when looking out over New York from the top of the Empire State Building?

2. Explain the **reciprocal** agreement between Dominion Bridge and the Mohawks.

3. Explain the initial wage **disparity** between the Mohawks and the skilled workers.

4. How do you know that the Mohawk workers were not simply showing **bravado** when they walked on high beams with nonchalance?

5. How would ironworkers atop a skyscraper appear to passing pedestrians?

6. What contribution did the Mohawks make to New York City?

7. What enabled many Mohawks to cease being **itinerant** workers?

advent
blasé
bravado
disparate
domicile
fabricate
itinerant
lilliputian
phobia
proclivity
projectile
queasy
reciprocate
relegate
vertigo

8. Where did the Mohawks go when the building boom in New York City ended?

9. When might a fear of heights be considered irrational?

10. How does a fear of heights manifest itself physically?

FUN & FASCINATING FACTS

Gulliver, the hero of Jonathan Swift's *Gulliver's Travels*, visits the land of Lilliput, whose inhabitants are tiny and to whom Gulliver appears gigantic. This work contributed the adjective **lilliputian** to the language. It can be spelled with a small or a capital *l*. A less common adjective, an antonym of *lilliputian*, is *Brobdingnagian*, derived from Swift's account of Gulliver's visit to Brobdingnag, a country of giants where everything is of immense size and where Gulliver seems tiny by comparison. *Brobdingnagian* is less common than *lilliputian* and because of this is still always capitalized.

The term **phobia**, from the Greek *phobos*, "fear," can stand alone to indicate a general fear or dislike; it can also occur in combination with a variety of Greek roots indicating various kinds of fear or hostility. *Acrophobia*, from the Greek *akros*, "topmost," is a fear of heights. *Xenophobia*, from the Greek *xenos*, "stranger," is a fear or hatred of what is strange or foreign. *Agoraphobia*, from the Greek *agora*, "marketplace," is a fear of open spaces. *Claustrophobia*, formed from the Latin *claustrum*, "an enclosed space," is a fear of being confined in a small or narrow space.

Lesson 10

Word List
Study the definitions of the words below; then do the exercises for the lesson.

amnesia
am nē´ zhə

n. 1. A loss of memory, usually caused by shock or injury.
The patient's **amnesia** was so acute that his own children were strangers to him.
2. A gap in one's memory.
While Uncle Rob had bad **amnesia** concerning his middle school years, he remembered his high school years perfectly.

appease
ə pēz´

v. 1. To bring to a state of peace or quiet.
The principal's reassurances did little to **appease** our concerns about the school's future.
2. To pacify an adversary, often by making concessions.
Attempts to **appease** dictators frequently serve only to increase their aggression.

attrition
ə trish´ ən

n. 1. A gradual reduction in numbers or loss of strength.
The **attrition** of manufacturing jobs in the United States was due in part to the rise of inexpensive imports.
2. A weakening resulting from pressure or harassment.
The guerrillas hid in the jungle and conducted a war of **attrition**.

debacle
de bäk´ əl

n. A sudden collapse, downfall, or failure.
A long rise in stock prices ended with the Wall Street **debacle** of 1929, which marked the advent of the Great Depression.

defoliate
dē fo´ lē āt

v. To strip a plant of leaves, thereby damaging or destroying it.
Gypsy moths **defoliated** many of the trees in the park, leaving bare branches in their wake.

equestrian
ē kwes´ trē ən

adj. Having to do with horseback riding.
Ana's love of horses led her to develop her **equestrian** skills.
n. One who rides on horseback.
An accomplished **equestrian** is usually familiar with the rules of show jumping.

expunge
ek spunj´

v. To obliterate or erase completely.
The burglar wiped the window sills, **expunging** any trace of his fingerprints.

hackneyed
hak´ nēd

adj. Commonplace; trite; lacking force or significance because of overuse.
"As cool as a cucumber" has become a **hackneyed** expression.

opprobrium
ə prō´ brē əm

n. Scornful treatment or contempt, especially as a result of disgraceful behavior.
Representative Michaels endured daily **opprobrium** in her district after being convicted of ethics violations.

proviso
prō vī´ zō

n. A statement that makes a condition, qualification, or restriction.
The Chowdry brothers accepted our invitation to dinner with the **proviso** that they be allowed to reciprocate.

sully
sul´ ē

v. To soil, tarnish, or besmirch.
Vandals had **sullied** the marble headstones with spray paint.

tactile tak´ tl	*adj.* Relating to or perceptible by the sense of touch. Braille employs **tactile** symbols that enable blind persons to read with their fingers.
upbraid up brād´	*v.* To scold or criticize severely; to find fault with. Mr. Hitzman was a martinet who often **upbraided** his students for not working hard enough.
verdant vʉrd´ nt	*adj.* Green with vegetation; covered with green plants. The Green Mountains are a fitting name for the **verdant** hills of Vermont.
vertex vʉr´ teks	*n.* The point opposite and farthest from the base; summit. The **vertex** of the Great Pyramid is 450 feet above the base.

10A Understanding Meanings

Read the sentences below. If a sentence correctly uses the word in bold, write *C* on the line below it. If a sentence is incorrect, rewrite it so that the vocabulary word in bold is used correctly.

1. A **verdant** valley is one full of growing plants.

_____

2. To **upbraid** someone is to offer that person encouragement.

_____

3. A **hackneyed** expression is one with a hidden meaning.

_____

4. An **equestrian** is a person who rides horseback.

_____

5. To **appease** someone is to do what is necessary to satisfy that person.

_____

6. A **defoliated** tree is one whose leaves have not yet opened up.

_____

7. A **tactile** response involves the sense of touch.

_____

8. A **proviso** is a promise made with no intention of keeping it.

9. To **expunge** a memory is to blot it out completely.

10. **Amnesia** is a state of bliss.

11. **Opprobrium** is strong disapproval.

12. To **sully** the beauty of something is to besmirch it.

13. **Attrition** is the lack of adequate nourishment.

14. A **vertex** is a mass of liquid whirling around a central point.

15. A **debacle** is a great disaster.

amnesia

appease

attrition

debacle

defoliate

equestrian

expunge

hackneyed

opprobrium

proviso

sully

tactile

upbraid

verdant

vertex

10B Using Words

If the word (or a form of the word) in bold fits in a sentence in the group below it, write the word in the blank space. If the word does not fit, leave the space empty.

1. **debacle**

   (a) Custer's 1876 Montana campaign ended in the _____ of the Little Bighorn.

   (b) The _____ of George McGovern's 1972 presidential defeat still rankles his Democratic supporters.

   (c) The prisoner's hands were locked in an iron _____ .

2. **sully**

   (a) I won't _____ you by repeating what he said about you.

   (b) The speaker attacked corporations who _____ the land by strip-mining it.

   (c) The many foundations of Rome have been _____ by years of air pollution.

3. **vertex**

   (a) The swirling _____ at the river's mouth threatened to capsize the boat.

   (b) Two sides of a triangle meet at its _____ .

   (c) From base to _____ , the Washington Monument is 555 feet, 5 inches.

4. **tactile**

   (a) The skin is an exquisitely sensitive _____ organ.

   (b) Bats have extremely _____ hearing and can fly in the dark by echolocation.

   (c) The _____ appeal of Aunt Janice's coat is such that one cannot resist stroking it.

5. **appease**

   (a) A sandwich and a piece of fruit were enough to _____ our hunger.

   (b) Britain and France attempted to _____ Hitler by giving in to his demands.

   (c) The wrath of the great khan was so monstrous that nothing could _____ it.

6. **defoliate**

   (a) When hair begins to _____ , there is little that one can do to prevent it.

   (b) Electric companies _____ the vegetation along the routes of power lines.

   (c) This exceptionally early winter will _____ many of Vermont's maple trees.

7. **upbraid**

   (a) Jenny asked her sister to help her _____ her hair.

   (b) I wanted to rush to your defense when I heard the coach _____ you for striking out.

   (c) The press continues to _____ Congress for its failure to pass the budget.

8. **expunge**

   (a) Soviet educators _____ all references to Trotsky in school history texts.

   (b) As the diaries were prepared for publication, many entries were _____ .

   (c) A tornado _____ the roof from our house.

10C Word Study

Each group of four words below contains two words that are either synonyms or antonyms. Circle these two words, then circle the *S* if they are synonyms or the *A* if they are antonyms.

1. nascent	incipient	eclectic	famous	S	A
2. abstruse	munificent	inveterate	stingy	S	A
3. equestrian	hackneyed	original	convivial	S	A
4. repulse	upbraid	sully	praise	S	A
5. comport	defoliate	appease	provoke	S	A
6. reciprocity	fabrication	discretion	falsehood	S	A
7. usurp	relinquish	deny	correlate	S	A
8. propitious	enthralled	enamored	hapless	S	A
9. abstruse	cavalier	absurd	recondite	S	A
10. presage	foreshadow	careen	expound	S	A

10D Images of Words

Circle the letter of each sentence that suggests the numbered bold vocabulary word. In each group, you may circle more than one letter or none at all.

amnesia
appease
attrition
debacle
defoliate
equestrian
expunge
hackneyed
opprobrium
proviso
sully
tactile
upbraid
verdant
vertex

1. **attrition**

   (a) The neighborhood residents were becoming healthier because of improved diets.

   (b) A series of storms had weakened the seawall to the point of collapse.

   (c) The agency reduced its size by not hiring replacements for retirees.

2. **hackneyed**

   (a) My painting teacher urged me to find a subject other than a ship in full sail.

   (b) The plot, involving aliens menacing the earth, was all too familiar.

   (c) Sharon's speech, on what she did last summer did not exactly break new ground.

3. **tactile**

   (a) It was comforting to feel Angela's hand in mine.

   (b) Miles had a strong feeling that the salesperson was not being honest with him.

   (c) The sculpture's curved surfaces felt smooth and cool.

4. **proviso**

   (a) I will complain to the manager, but only if you agree to come with me.

   (b) If you don't drive the car out of state, you can rent it at a lower rate.

   (c) I provided the children with everything they would need for their trip to the ballgame.

5. **verdant**

   (a) Betsy was green with envy when she heard I'd won first prize in the Science Fair.

   (b) The neighborhood lawns were lush after the spring rains.

   (c) It was a fine summer day with not a cloud in the sky.

6. **equestrian**

   (a) Lawrence of Arabia's skill at riding a camel impressed his Arab hosts.

   (b) The painting shows General Lee mounted on his favorite horse, Traveller.

   (c) Dressage is the guiding of a horse through a complex series of maneuvers.

7. **appease**

   (a) The Epsteins promised to take their children to see the Grand Canyon.

   (b) Mrs. Kerner gave her rambunctious son a new action figure to keep him quiet.

   (c) The Canadian government gave in to Quebec's demands for special status.

8. **opprobrium**

   (a) I was thrilled when my boss complimented me on doing such a good job.

   (b) He was ostracized after his perjury became public.

   (c) Even though she repaid her client for the money she used improperly, the lawyer was still shunned by some of her colleagues.

9. **amnesia**

   (a) I forgot to pick up the dry cleaning on my way home from work.

   (b) Mr. Waite has no memory of the events that occurred prior to his head injury.

   (c) Herr Kraus claims to have no memory of his participation in the Nazi party.

10. **upbraid**

    (a) My teammates tried to cheer me up after my fumble lost us the game.

    (b) For an extra twenty dollars we were able to travel first-class.

    (c) The report is out of date and needs to be completely rewritten.

10E Passage

Read the passage below; then complete the exercise that follows it.

The Wall

The Vietnam War had devastating repercussions for millions of Americans and others involved in the conflict. It began innocuously enough in 1956 when American military advisers were sent to South Vietnam to aid its government against the communist opposition, who were themselves supported by North Vietnam— already governed by a communist regime. By the late 1960s, the United States was deeply involved in what had become a war of **attrition**, measured by daily "body counts" as each side hoped to exhaust the other into giving up. Fifty-eight thousand Americans died in the war and almost a third of a million were wounded. As many as two million Vietnamese lives may have been lost, including those of many thousands of civilians. The country was devastated by intensive bombing and by highly toxic chemical **defoliation** intended to eliminate the cover of trees and other vegetation. The war is estimated to have cost U.S. taxpayers about two hundred billion dollars. It ended in 1975 with a North Vietnamese victory.

A total of 2.7 million American men and women had served in Vietnam. As they returned home, a planeload at a time, they were not generally given the hero's welcome that Americans returning from previous wars had received. Instead, they were met by a public deeply divided over the merits of the war. Many Americans found it difficult to show support for those who had fought in a war they believed was wrong, even though most veterans had been compelled to serve. Some soldiers were even **upbraided** as war criminals and murderers by extreme opponents of the war. Veterans were hurt and confused by the **opprobrium** they encountered.

Some retreated into silence but were unable to **expunge** the horrific experiences of the war from their memories. In contrast, a public **amnesia** regarding the war developed. Many Americans were unwilling to confront the war's many painful issues: its tremendous human and material costs, the animosity between its opponents and supporters, and the fact that the American side was defeated.

In the late 1970s, veterans of the Vietnam War started a fund for construction of a memorial to those who had died. They raised nearly nine million dollars through private donations and held a competition to select a design for it, with the **proviso** that the memorial express no political view of the war.

Maya Lin was a twenty-one-year-old architecture student at Yale University when one of her professors required that his students submit a proposal for the design competition for the memorial. The popular conception of a war memorial recalled the heroic **equestrian** statues of Civil War generals, but in Lin's opinion, such **hackneyed** representations were a simplification of the war. Her design called for two triangular walls of polished black granite to be built into the earth, set in the shape of a shallow V. Carved into the stone would be the names of all the men and women killed in the war or still missing, in chronological order by the date of their death or disappearance. The wall would increase in height as one descended until, at its **vertex**, where the trench is deepest, it would be ten feet high. Visitors to the memorial would be able to run their fingers over the names of loved ones. This **tactile** quality was to become an important aspect of Lin's work.

Congress had chosen a **verdant** stretch of ground between the Lincoln Memorial and the Capitol as the site of the memorial, and in the spring of 1981, the judges of the competition, after evaluating the 1,421 entries, declared Maya Lin's proposal the winner. The vote was unanimous, but the public's reaction to the design, reflecting their ambivalence about the war itself, was sharply divided. Those opposing it called it "a degrading ditch" and "a wall of shame" that **sullied** the memory of those who had died. They wanted a memorial that would honor the dead. To **appease** the critics, a bronze statue of three larger-than-life soldiers was placed near the entrance, and a second statue, of three servicewomen, was added later.

Despite the initial criticism, Lin's wall, dedicated in 1982, has been a focal point for national discussion of the war. The memorial draws over a million visitors a year, more than any other site in the nation's capital, and is a powerful tribute to the fallen, from Harry C. Cramer, an army captain killed during a training action in 1957, to Richard Vande Geer, killed on May 15, 1975,

amnesia

appease

attrition

debacle

defoliate

equestrian

expunge

hackneyed

opprobrium

proviso

sully

tactile

upbraid

verdant

vertex

during the **debacle** of the war's final days as the last Americans fled the country. Many are moved to tears by their visit. Lin has said that the wall "was not meant to be cheerful or happy, but to bring out in people the realization of loss and a cathartic healing process." Perhaps she has succeeded in her aim.

Answer each of the following questions in the form of a sentence. If a question does not contain a vocabulary word from this lesson's word list, use one in your answer. Use each word only once.

1. Why is it unlikely that Vietnam was very **verdant** at the end of the war?

2. How do you know the war did not end in **appeasement**?

3. Why is the war called "a war of **attrition**"?

4. What is suggested by the statement that "a public **amnesia** regarding the war developed"?

5. How do you know that many American civilians felt **opprobrium** for the war?

6. Where would the names of those who died at the war's midpoint be found?

7. Why do you think Maya Lin incorporated a **tactile** quality into her design?

8. What was wrong with Lin's memorial in the eyes of her critics?

9. What details in the passage suggest that it was impossible to fulfill the **proviso** that the monument express no political view of the war?

10. Is it possible that Lin's idea for the memorial could become **hackneyed**? Explain your answer.

FUN & FASCINATING FACTS

The Greek *mnestos* means "remembered" and combines with the Greek prefix *a-*, "not," to form **amnesia**. A person suffering from this condition cannot remember. Several other words share this root. If a government grants *amnesty* for a crime, it is indicating a willingness to forget about it, to refrain from prosecution. A *mnemonic* (the initial *m* is silent) is an aid in remembering, such as a rhyme or acronym.

A *hackney* was once a horse rented to anyone wishing to hire it. Later, the word was applied to a horse pulling a coach that was for hire. The term probably originated in Hackney, a district of London, where such horses were raised. A **hackneyed** horse was one that had become worn out through excessive use. The term was then applied to verbal expressions or ideas that were similarly worn out through overuse.

Lesson 11

Word List
Study the definitions of the words below; then do the exercises for the lesson.

attenuate
ə ten′ yо̄о̄ āt

v. 1. To make or become thin.
By twisting and pulling, the spinner can **attenuate** the mass of wool fibers into a long slender thread.
2. To lessen the amount, force, or value of.
That stone breakwater **attenuates** the impact of high storm tides on this harbor.

behemoth
bē hē′ məth

n. Something or someone of enormous size or power.
The Warriors' new linebacker is a 300-pound **behemoth** whose size alone intimidates his opponents.

disinter
dis in tur′

v. To remove from a grave or tomb; to dig up.
The remains of the Russian royal family were **disinterred** from their unmarked grave and given a proper burial.

impinge
im pinj′

(Used with *on*) *v.* 1. To go beyond desirable or established limits; to encroach.
The proposed law would **impinge** on citizens' freedom to choose their own health-care provider.
2. To come into contact with, especially forcefully.
A blinding flash **impinged** on my field of vision.

multifarious
mul tə far′ ē əs

adj. Having many forms; varied, versatile.
The **multifarious** sounds of the city created a discordant noise.

oxymoron
äk si môr′ än

n. A combination of words that seem to be contradictory.
"Make haste slowly" is a bit of advice that is an **oxymoron**.

plenitude
ple′ nə то̄о̄d

n. An ample amount; an abundance.
Our successful radio appeal yielded a **plenitude** of volunteers for the beach cleanup.

postulate
päs′ chə lāt

v. To assume as a fact based on the best available evidence.
Following the discovery of several ancient skeletons in Africa, archaeologists **postulated** that *Homo sapiens* is descended from African ancestors.
n. (päs′ chə lat) Something assumed to be self-evident; a fundamental principle.
It is a **postulate** of diplomacy that nations are motivated by self-interest.

prevail
prē vāl′

v. 1. To prove superior in power or strength.
Good usually **prevails** over evil in the movies.
2. To remain in effect or use; to be current or widespread.
Low gasoline prices have **prevailed** for the past few years due to the cheapness of crude oil.

putrefy
pyо̄о̄′ trə fī

v. To become rotten or decayed, giving off a foul odor.
The carcasses **putrefied** and attracted scavengers.

salubrious
sə lо̄о̄′ brē əs

adj. Beneficial to health or well-being.
The **salubrious** mountain air renewed the hikers' vigor.

succulent suk´ yo͞o lənt	*adj.* Fresh and juicy. Juice from the **succulent** peach dribbled down my chin.
tundra tun´ drə	*n.* Flat, treeless plains of the arctic regions. The main vegetation of the cold **tundra** consists of mosses, lichens, and small flowering plants.
unequivocal un ē kwiv´ ə kəl	*adj.* Leaving no room for misunderstanding; unambiguous. When I asked to borrow their new car, my parents replied with an **unequivocal** no.
vicissitudes vi sis´ ə to͞odz	*n.* pl. Fluctuations in conditions; changes of fortune. The **vicissitudes** of Lincoln's life are fully explored in this new biography.

11A Understanding Meanings

Read the sentences below. If a sentence correctly uses the word in bold, write *C* on the line below it. If a sentence is incorrect, rewrite it so that the vocabulary word in bold is used correctly.

1. To **disinter** something is to dig it out of the ground.

_____

2. To **prevail** is to overcome.

_____

3. A **behemoth** is a lilliputian creature.

_____

4. **Multifarious** activities are those of great diversity or variety.

_____

5. **Vicissitudes** are firmly rooted attitudes that are difficult to alter.

_____

6. To **impinge** on something is to come into contact with it.

_____

7. The **tundra** is the area on a coast between the high and low tides.

_____

attenuate
behemoth
disinter
impinge
multifarious
oxymoron
plenitude
postulate
prevail
putrefy
salubrious
succulent
tundra
unequivocal
vicissitudes

8. An **unequivocal** statement is one that can be taken in just one way.

9. To **putrefy** is to feel queasy.

10. Something that is **succulent** is juicy.

11. A **postulate** is a statement that is assumed to be the truth.

12. To **attenuate** something is to pay attention to it.

13. An **oxymoron** is a statement that appears to be self-contradictory.

14. A **salubrious** regimen is one that is beneficial to one's health.

15. A **plenitude** of applicants is an ample number of them.

11B Using Words

If the word (or a form of the word) in bold fits a sentence in the group below it, write the word in the blank. If the word does not fit, leave the space empty.

1. **impinge**

   (a) The soft rain made no sound as it _____ on the roof.

   (b) Trouble erupted when European colonies began to _____ on native lands.

   (c) You are entitled to enjoy your rights provided they do not _____ on mine.

2. **prevail**

    (a) Ancient customs still _____ among the Kayapo people of Brazil's Amazon region.

    (b) Higher temperatures are expected to _____ over most of the region.

    (c) Some people had doubts about whether the Union would _____ over the Confederacy.

3. **unequivocal**

    (a) The contest was so _____ that its outcome was a foregone conclusion.

    (b) Is this _____ promise, which was put in writing, legally binding?

    (c) Both sides have taken _____ positions on the question of legal reform.

4. **succulent**

    (a) These sauteed mushrooms wrapped in pastry are _____ morsels.

    (b) You have to be pretty _____ to hand over your life's savings to strangers.

    (c) A basket of _____ tropical fruits makes a wonderful gift.

5. **disinter**

    (a) Ms. Olach claimed that as a _____ observer she could provide the most accurate information about what happened.

    (b) Scientists at the site have _____ an entire stegosaurus skeleton.

    (c) Your mention of these old disputes has _____ me a great deal.

6. **attenuate**

    (a) Our proximity to the ocean _____ the harshness of winter.

    (b) The Republicans' control of Congress has _____ the president's power.

    (c) Gold can be _____ into wire so fine that it is almost invisible.

7. **putrefy**

    (a) In hot weather, meat left unrefrigerated will soon _____ .

    (b) When exposed to warm air, an ice cube will _____ .

    (c) An open wound will _____ if left untreated.

8. **tundra**

    (a) It took us a week to cross the African _____ in our four-wheel drive vehicle.

    (b) Rock ptarmigans and arctic hares share the _____ of Ellsmere Island, which lies only 480 miles from the North Pole.

    (c) The _____ lies between the arctic icecap and the northern tree line.

attenuate
behemoth
disinter
impinge
multifarious
oxymoron
plenitude
postulate
prevail
putrefy
salubrious
succulent
tundra
unequivocal
vicissitudes

11C Word Study

Complete the analogies by selecting the pair of words whose relationship most resembles the relationship of the pair in capital letters. Circle the letter in front of the pair you choose.

1. ARCHIPELAGO : ISLAND ::
   (a) hand : finger
   (b) loaf : bread
   (c) grove : tree
   (d) boat : water

2. ETYMOLOGY : WORDS ::
   (a) fauna : animals
   (b) soliloquy : drama
   (c) penitence : salubrious
   (d) botany : plants

3. VOTARY : CAUSE ::
   (a) mortification : shame
   (b) behemoth : monstrosity
   (c) patrician : wealth
   (d) patriot : nation

4. RENEGADE : LOYALTY ::
   (a) martinet : discipline
   (b) scoundrel : probity
   (c) fool : folly
   (d) raconteur : humor

5. COURAGE : BRAVADO ::
   (a) confidence : arrogance
   (b) daydream : reverie
   (c) shortage : surfeit
   (d) levity : laughter

6. EQUESTRIAN : HORSES ::
   (a) incremental : increases
   (b) seismic : earthquakes
   (c) therapeutic : diseases
   (d) penitent : wrongdoers

7. TACTILE : TOUCH ::
   (a) vibrant : health
   (b) eclectic : choice
   (c) unsavory : taste
   (d) visual : sight

8. VERDANT : COLOR ::
   (a) blasé : confidence
   (b) multifarious : plenitude
   (c) octagonal : shape
   (d) multifarious : variety

9. TUNDRA : GEOGRAPHY ::
   (a) telescope : astronomy
   (b) plan : architecture
   (c) paragraph : story
   (d) equation : mathematics

10. VICISSITUDES : LIFE ::
   (a) gesticulations : movement
   (b) accoutrements : equipment
   (c) fluctuations : temperature
   (d) emoluments : payment

11D Images of Words

Circle the letter of each sentence that suggests the numbered bold vocabulary word. In each group, you may circle more than one letter or none at all.

1. **salubrious**

   (a) Dr. Connor's comments on women caused much offense to those who heard them.

   (b) Arizona's climate is ideal for those who suffer from respiratory ills.

   (c) The arts in Florence prospered under Lorenzo de' Medici's patronage.

2. **unequivocal**

   (a) When Anita baby-sits, she rarely allows her charges to stay up past their bedtime.

   (b) Amanda's usual response to a direct question was, "Well, yes and no."

   (c) The Senate voted 100 to 0 in favor of making apple pie the national dish.

3. **multifarious**

   (a) A chessboard is made up of sixty-four contrasting squares.

   (b) The city's problems multiply alarmingly, yet little is done about them.

   (c) Dana was amazed at how many skills are required to run a farm.

4. **impinge**

   (a) Anyone interfering with play by running onto the field can be prosecuted.

   (b) The college's expansion plan involves taking over most of the neighboring area.

   (c) Ms. Calvino received so many phone calls that she had no time to work on her book.

5. **succulent**

   (a) It happened that I could not have chosen a better time to ask the question.

   (b) The lifestyles of rich people had a powerful attraction for Allen.

   (c) The sugar maples were ablaze with vibrant reds and golds.

6. **postulate**

   (a) Newton presumed a link between planetary orbits and a falling apple.

   (b) Let us suppose that the moon is in fact made of cheese.

   (c) The evidence suggests that the first hominids appeared several million years ago.

7. **behemoth**

   (a) This small, winged creature is similar to a butterfly.

   (b) Brachiosaurus, weighing 80 tons, lived 150 million years ago.

   (c) The newest aircraft carrier to join the U.S. fleet is the largest vessel afloat.

attenuate
behemoth
disinter
impinge
multifarious
oxymoron
plenitude
postulate
prevail
putrefy
salubrious
succulent
tundra
unequivocal
vicissitudes

8. **plenitude**

   (a) This year's apple harvest is the biggest in many years.

   (b) Over 500 species of butterfly live in Thailand's tropical rain forest.

   (c) Charlemagne is said to have stood six and a half feet tall.

9. **vicissitudes**

   (a) Danny Delgado had made and lost several fortunes before he was forty.

   (b) The economy has had its ups and downs in the last twenty years.

   (c) During March, it rained every day, making it the wettest month on record.

10. **oxymoron**

   (a) As to what will happen in the future, I remain cheerfully pessimistic.

   (b) The proposal to increase taxes was greeted with a deafening silence.

   (c) The old proverb advises us that haste makes waste.

11E Passage

Read the passage below; then complete the exercise that follows it.

Dwarf Mammoths

Before the early 1990s, reference books asserted **unequivocally** that the ancestral elephants known as mammoths had become extinct about ten thousand years ago at the end of the Ice Age, a period that lasted one and a half million years, but was marked by periodic advances and retreats of the great polar ice sheet.

Scientists speculate that mammoths may have grown gradually to such a great size as a means of defense. A **multifarious** array of predators, including wolves, saber-toothed tigers, and even lions, had adapted to the harsh climate **prevailing** along the edge of the ice sheet. But for any of these, preying on such a **behemoth** of an animal would have been a formidable undertaking. Because there was a **plenitude** of less imposing animals sharing the same grazing land, whose meat was just as **succulent**, mammoths were often ignored.

The warming trend that caused the most recent retreat of the ice sheet resulted in rising sea levels and a dramatically changed climate—one much less **salubrious** for many of the animals then living, including the mammoth with its four-inch-thick layer of fat and long, shaggy coat. The overall temperature rose and the amount of rainfall increased. The once rich, dry grasslands became soggy **tundra** with little plant life. The mammoth was left with much less vegetation on which to feed. And yet this was not the first major climatic change that this creature had encountered. Even though the polar ice cap had advanced and retreated four or five times over the course of the Ice Age, the mammoth had survived these **vicissitudes**. The difference this time was the arrival of an unfamiliar predator more intelligent than any it had faced before.

The end of the Ice Age made it possible for human beings to extend the range of their activity; they began **impinging** on the mammoth's northern habitat. In addition, they found this huge animal very useful. It provided hunters venturing that far north with food, clothing, and even shelter. Its curving twelve-foot tusks could be formed into a framework that when covered with skins became a domed hut. The mammoth population, already thinned by the decrease in its food supply, ill adapted to the newly warmer climate, and hunted increasingly by humans, gradually lost the battle for survival. The population became **attenuated** until, ten thousand years ago, the species became extinct.

Or so it was believed. Then in March of 1993, a Russian research team announced that fragments of mammoth bone and tusk together with a number of teeth had been dug up a few years earlier on an island about 100 miles off the coast of northeastern Siberia. That in itself was unremarkable. Entire mammoth carcasses have been **disinterred** from the frigid wilderness of Alaska and Siberia. Deep frozen for ten thousand years, the meat from such carcasses had escaped the **putrefying** effects of air and water and was actually still edible, though perhaps not very palatable. What startled the scientific community now was the discovery that some of the teeth that belonged to normal-sized mammoths of ten to fourteen feet height were around thirteen to twenty thousand years old, while teeth from adult mammoths scarcely six feet tall were four to seven thousand years old. Was it possible that these were midgets of the species?

The term "dwarf mammoth" is an **oxymoron**, but the evidence that such a creature existed was indisputable and the explanation intriguing. Wrangel Island, where the fragments were found, was formed when the sea level rose at the end of the Ice Age, isolating the island mammoths from those on the mainland. The porous rock on Wrangel allowed for good drainage, so that the fertile soil produced abundant vegetation. Scientists **postulate** that with no predators and a limited grazing area, there was no longer much survival value to be gained from great size. The evidence indicates that over a period of about six thousand years, succeeding generations of island mammoths gradually became smaller until their height was less than half that of their ancestors. What happened to the last generation of dwarf mammoths, 4,000 years ago, is not known for certain. But because scientists know that humans visited Wrangel Island, they conjecture that the dwarf mammoths, like their mainland relatives, were hunted to extinction.

Answer each of the following questions in the form of a sentence. If a question does not contain a vocabulary word from this lesson's word list, use one in your answer. Use each word only once.

1. Why does the **tundra** provide poor grazing for animals?

_____

2. Why did mammoths grow to such a large size?

_____

3. Why is the phrase "a dwarf mammoth" an **oxymoron**?

_____

attenuate

behemoth   4. How did the melting of the ice cap **impinge** on the survival of the mammoth in most places?

disinter

impinge   _____

multifarious

oxymoron   5. Why was this climate change **salubrious** for mammoths on Wrangel Island?

plenitude

postulate   _____

prevail

putrefy   6. How did humans use the mammoths after they killed them?

salubrious

succulent   _____

tundra

unequivocal

vicissitudes

7. Why would it be inaccurate to say that **disinterring** the mammoth remains on Wrangel Island was a very unpleasant task for the researchers?

8. Give two additional reasons why mammoths thrived on Wrangel Island.

9. Why should scientists be wary of making **unequivocal** statements?

FUN & FASCINATING FACTS

The Book of Job in the Old Testament makes reference to **Behemoth**, a creature of enormous size but otherwise unidentified. Scholars believe it to have been a hippopotamus. The word entered the language to describe anything of great size or power; it is written with a capital *b* only when referring to the Biblical animal.

By definition and usage, **oxymoron** and *oxygen* would seem to be completely unrelated words— but they do share a common prefix, the Greek *oxy-*, "sharp, acid, pointed." When combined with the Greek root *moros*, "dull, stupid, foolish," it yields a word meaning "pointedly or acutely foolish," which an obviously contradictory term like "jumbo shrimp" seems to be. *Oxygen* shares the prefix because early chemists thought the gas was instrumental in the formation of acids. The French *oxygène* originally meant "acidifying agent."

Lesson 12

Word List

Study the definitions of the words below; then do the exercises for the lesson.

amity
am´ i tē

n. Peaceful relations; friendship.
Student groups that had once opposed each other were able to work together with **amity** to design the new after-school program.

animadversion
a nəm ad vər´ zhən

n. (Usually used with *on*.) A critical or hostile comment.
Drew was disconsolate after reading the critics' **animadversions** on her latest novel.

antithetical
an tə the´ ti kəl

adj. Being in direct and outspoken opposition.
The poet employed antithetical symbols such as those of birth and death.
antithesis *n.* (an tith´ ə sis) The direct contrast of one thing with another; the exact opposite.
Kyla's munificence is the **antithesis** of her brother's stinginess.

bellicose
bel´ i kōs

adj. Inclined to quarrel; combative; warlike.
The principal upbraided the students for their **bellicose** behavior.

bucolic
byōō käl´ ik

adj. Of or relating to country life; rustic; pastoral.
Li-chen was reluctant to leave the **bucolic** environs of his grandparents' farm.

craven
krā´ vən

adj. Utterly lacking courage; willing to give up or capitulate.
Too **craven** to oppose the dictator, the country's elite tried desperately to appease him.

exalt
eg zôlt´

v. To raise in rank, wealth, or honor; to praise highly; glorify.
The Roman senate **exalted** the emperor Caligula by declaring him a god.
exalted *adj.*
By knighting Laurence Olivier in 1947, King George VI placed him in the **exalted** ranks of those who have given great service to England.

impugn
im pyōōn´

v. To attack as false; to call into question.
By accusing him of financial improprieties, the committee **impugned** the treasurer's honesty.

introspective
in trə spek´ tiv

adj. Inclined to look inward and examine one's thoughts and feelings.
Nadine's **introspective** nature was in sharp contrast to her sister's gregarious personality.
introspection *n.*
After days of careful **introspection**, Alexis chose which college she would attend.

metier
me´ tyā

(A French word now part of our vocabulary.) *n.* Work or activity for which one is particularly suited.
After earning a law degree, Chitra realized that her real **metier** was writing novels.

penurious
pe nyōōr´ ē əs

adj. 1. Marked by extreme poverty.
The family had once been wealthy, but now lived a **penurious** life.
2. Stingy; lacking generosity.
Despite his hoard of gold, Silas Marner was **penurious**, sharing his money with no one.
penury *n.* (pen´ yə rē)
Mrs. Nakamura always appeared in her finest clothes, as if to conceal her **penury**.

privation prī vā´ shən	*n.* An instance or condition of extreme hardship; a lack of comfort. The lost hikers suffered many **privations** in the weeks before their rescue.
sobriquet sō´ bri kā	(A French word now part of our vocabulary.) *n.* A nickname. Although her name was Claudia, the First Lady was known by the **sobriquet** "Lady Bird" Johnson.
tantamount tant´ ə mount	*n.* Equivalent to; the same as. "Refusing to support the bill is **tantamount** to voting against it," bellowed the senator.
throes thrōz	*n.* pl. Conditions of painful or difficult change, struggle, or turmoil. Economists offered a plenitude of explanations as to why the country was in the **throes** of recession.

12A Understanding Meanings

Read the sentences below. If a sentence correctly uses the word in bold, write *C* on the line below it. If a sentence is incorrect, rewrite it so that the vocabulary word in bold is used correctly.

1. **Penury** is the price one pays for doing something wrong.

_____

2. An **introspective** person is one who reflects on her acts and motives.

_____

3. To **impugn** someone's honesty is to affirm it.

_____

4. Someone's **metier** is an area of activity in which that person excels.

_____

5. **Throes** are circumstances of struggle or difficulty.

_____

6. To **exalt** something is to elevate its status.

_____

7. A **bucolic** scene is one that suggests placid country life.

_____

8. **Privation** is a desire to be alone.

9. An **antithesis** is something that is a sharp contrast.

10. A **craven** act is one that fulfills a strong desire.

11. An **animadversion** is a strong dislike.

12. To be **tantamount** to something is to be almost the same as it.

13. A **sobriquet** is an expression of joy.

14. A **bellicose** person is one who likes to fight.

15. **Amity** is a state of friendly relations.

amity
animadversion
antithetical
bellicose
bucolic
craven
exalt
impugn
introspective
metier
penurious
privation
sobriquet
tantamount
throes

12B Using Words

If the word (or a form of the word) in bold fits in a sentence in the group below it, write the word in the blank space. If the word does not fit, leave the space empty.

1. **exalt**

(a) The advent of conflict _____ the Defense Department above all other cabinet departments.

(b) Those who _____ wealth often discovered it could not buy happiness.

(c) Phillips holds an _____ opinion of her value to the company.

2. **introspective**

    (a) In a series of _____ poems, Dickinson meditates on life's vicissitudes.

    (b) The gallery's _____ exhibition includes all of the painter's major works.

    (c) In an _____ mood, Mel contemplated his career possibilities.

3. **throes**

    (a) Because we were in the _____ of moving, I had no opportunity to say goodbye.

    (b) By the late 1980s, Eastern Europe was in the _____ of a political change.

    (c) I have so many _____ requiring my attention that I cannot help you.

4. **tantamount**

    (a) It is of _____ importance that the director gets the message without delay.

    (b) Leaking these secret documents is _____ to treason.

    (c) Bending the truth to that extent is _____ to lying.

5. **bucolic**

    (a) The heavy meal had made us _____ and incapable of serious exertion.

    (b) Dr. McGee yearned for the _____ life of a gentleman farmer.

    (c) Muir's journals were resplendent with the _____ imagery of the country.

6. **impugn**

    (a) Lina's comments were not designed to _____ your honesty.

    (b) To _____ another's honor once meant risking a duel.

    (c) Failure to maintain the engine is bound to _____ its performance.

7. **penurious**

    (a) Although Ms. Atwood is now a wealthy woman, hers was a _____ childhood.

    (b) Ebenezer Scrooge finally saw the error of his _____ ways.

    (c) The land is so _____ that few crops will grow on it.

8. **antithetical**

    (a) The candidate's views are _____ to those in the party platform.

    (b) The raconteur used the _____ symbols of fire and ice in her tale.

    (c) My parents are _____ to my getting an apartment.

12C Word Study

Choose from the two words provided and use each word only once when filling in the spaces. One space should be left blank.

expunge/erase

1. A presidential pardon can _____ a person's criminal conviction.

2. The five of us got together to _____ the damage done by the hurricane.

3. It's easy to _____ a document on your computer without meaning to.

advent/arrival

4. We're told the train's _____ has been delayed a further thirty minutes.

5. Until the _____ of writing, there could be no recorded history.

6. Delilah made her _____ on the London stage to prolonged applause.

craven /cowardly

7. The ordinary people had to suffer a great deal because of the _____ behavior of their spineless leaders.

8. The _____ lion is a lovable character in *The Wizard of Oz*.

9. The _____ twist to his mouth when he smirked annoyed me.

postulate/assume

10. The hotel manager told us we could not _____ our room without a deposit.

11. Don't _____ she's coming back just because she left without saying goodbye.

12. Let us _____ that global warming continues at its present rate.

phobia/fear

13. A _____ of snakes is probably a healthy attribute in humans.

14. One way to treat a _____ is with something called "aversion therapy."

15. The _____ seemed to come from inside the old oak chest.

amity
animadversion
antithetical
bellicose
bucolic
craven
exalt
impugn
introspective
metier
penurious
privation
sobriquet
tantamount
throes

12D Images of Words

Circle the letter of each sentence that suggests the numbered bold vocabulary word. In each group, you may circle more than one letter or none at all.

1. **bellicose**

   (a) Some European nations have too often resorted to war to settle their differences.

   (b) The company is looking for salespeople who are competitive and aggressive.

   (c) "Fifty-four forty or fight" was the Democrats' slogan in the 1844 election.

2. **craven**

   (a) The mere sight of the ice cream parlor makes Meg long for a sundae.

   (b) I was appalled by how easily Gina's parents caved in to her strident demands.

   (c) The opposition candidate charged the incumbent governor with consistently lacking the courage to fight for his programs.

3. **privation**

   (a) Homeless people are forced to live on the street if shelters are full.

   (b) The star athlete's house was surrounded by an eight-foot wall to keep out the curious.

   (c) During the Great Depression, families often went without food.

4. **amity**

   (a) The motion to change the group's name was defeated by 104 votes to 103.

   (b) The legend tells of a golden age when all nations lived in peace.

   (c) The two families lived together, never speaking an angry word.

5. **metier**

   (a) Joe's first job after graduation was at a fast-food restaurant.

   (b) Although she never gave up playing the piano, the trumpet was Billie's great love.

   (c) Unlike many politicians, the senator from Texas thrived on campaigning.

6. **penury**

   (a) Frank stared at the questions, unable to answer a single one.

   (b) Susan spent her money only on that which she needed.

   (c) Charles had been in failing health for some time, but remained cheerful.

7. **sobriquet**

   (a) Catherine was mortified when her friends began calling her "Kitty."

   (b) The proud parents named the child Oscar Fingal O'Flahertie Wills Wilde.

   (c) Britain's Prime Minister Thatcher was once dubbed the "Iron Lady."

8. **bucolic**

    (a) The voyage passed uneventfully and was marked by unusually calm seas.

    (b) Cindy was content, curled up in her favorite armchair with a good book.

    (c) The country was at peace and its people prospered.

9. **animadversion**

    (a) Sally told us about the time she went riding and her horse suddenly bolted.

    (b) Emma chose to ignore Sam's comment that she was too clumsy to be a serious dancer.

    (c) As soon as Paul moved his bishop, he saw that he had fallen into a trap.

10. **antithesis**

    (a) Communism promised the Russian people a worker's paradise but resulted in economic disaster.

    (b) The new mayor reversed all of the policies begun by his predecessor.

    (c) The topic of Jesse's term paper was "Historical arguments against slavery."

12E Passage

Read the passage below; then complete the exercise that follows it.

A Child of the Sixties

Entertainers hoping to enhance their popularity by avoiding controversy often keep quiet on divisive issues of the day; to express strong opinions may risk offending those who hold **antithetical** views. But throughout her long career, folk singer Joan Baez has willingly risked her reputation, her profession, and sometimes her life fighting for peace and social justice.

Her first album, released in 1960, coincided with the beginning of one of the most tumultuous decades in American history. It was a time when the United States was in the **throes** of a civil rights revolution at home while fighting an increasingly unpopular war in Vietnam. Dr. Martin Luther King, Jr. was leading protest marches and addressing rallies throughout the South; students were burning draft cards and going to jail for refusing to serve in the armed forces, acts considered courageous by supporters and **craven** by critics.

In 1963, when Dr. King delivered the historic "I Have a Dream" speech in Washington, D.C., Joan Baez was there to lead the crowd of several hundred thousand in singing the civil rights anthem "We Shall Overcome." When Dr. King led protests against racial injustice, she marched with him. She was also active in the antiwar movement. Like many people who vigorously protested against the Vietnam War, Joan Baez was arrested and sent to jail.

This deep desire for justice and change was embodied by Woodstock, a three-day music festival held at a **bucolic** upstate New York farm in 1969. Young people from across America came together at Woodstock in a spirit of **amity** and love to celebrate the ideals of the decade. Baez was there as well, voicing her convictions in song. If anyone deserves the **sobriquet** "Child of the Sixties," it is Joan Baez.

In December 1972, Baez and three other Americans visited North Vietnam just as the United States grew more **bellicose**, stepping up its bombing attacks. During their thirteen-day stay, these visitors shared the **privations** of the Vietnamese people in makeshift shelters as the bombs rained down—a gesture that was regarded by Baez's critics as **tantamount** to treason.

amity
animadversion
antithetical
bellicose
bucolic
craven
exalt
impugn
introspective
metier
penurious
privation
sobriquet
tantamount
throes

Baez was born in 1941 to a Scottish-American mother and a Mexican-American father. Joan went to school in a middle-class southern California community with a substantial Hispanic population. Because she spoke only English, the Hispanic children at school avoided her, while the white children would have nothing to do with her because she looked Hispanic. The isolation she suffered made her **introspective**, but also gave her the strength to be self-reliant, a quality that her parents encouraged in all three of their daughters.

Music provided a way for the shy young girl to reach out to others. She was blessed with what one critic has called "an achingly pure soprano" voice. She bought her first guitar at age fifteen and began singing at school gatherings. Audiences responded enthusiastically, and the young musician knew she had found her **metier**. The family moved to the Boston area following Joan's graduation from high school. Soon she began singing in local coffeehouses. Within three years her concerts were regularly sold out, her albums were best-sellers, and her picture was on the cover of *Time* magazine. She had joined the **exalted** ranks of elite musicians but did not abandon her ideals.

Joan Baez used her fame to draw attention to the causes she championed and gave them financial as well as personal support. Critics who did not share her views were quick to **impugn** her sincerity, perhaps in the belief that people should be **penurious** themselves when speaking out on behalf of the poor and downtrodden. She ignored their **animadversions** and carried on doing what she had always done—singing and campaigning tirelessly for an array of social justice causes. In a 1998 interview, Joan Baez looked back on a professional career of more than four decades that had produced over forty albums. She was also looking ahead, she said, anticipating the day when she would stop singing professionally and devote her time to social activism, prose writing, or just catching her breath. Happily for her many fans, she keeps postponing that day. In 2002, she began yet another national tour. Its purpose? To promote the careers of young musicians.

Answer each of the following questions in the form of a sentence. If a question does not contain a vocabulary word from this lesson's word list, use one in your answer. Use each word only once.

1. What aspects of American life did Dr. King **impugn**?

_____

2. Would you use the word **amity** to describe the atmosphere of the 1960s? Why or why not?

_____

3. Why would those who wanted more **bellicose** actions taken in Vietnam have felt out of place at Woodstock?

_____

4. In what way did Baez expose herself to **privations**?

_____

5. For what reasons did Baez experience **animadversions** during her career?

_____

6. How did Joan Baez's 1960s activism contrast with her outlook as a child?

_____

7. How do you know that Baez probably did not have a **penurious** childhood?

8. In your view, what is Baez's **metier**?

9. Why would it be inaccurate to describe Baez as **craven** in her political views?

10. In your view, what does the **sobriquet** "Child of the Sixties" mean?

FUN & FASCINATING FACTS

When people meet in a spirit of **amity**, they do so in a friendly manner. The root of this word comes from the Latin *amicus*, "friend." Several other words share this root. An *amiable* person is one who is friendly. To settle a dispute *amicably* is to do so in a friendly manner. In legal terminology, an *amicus curiae*, literally "a friend of the court," is a person who is allowed to advise the court, but has no stake in the outcome of the case.

Bellicose denotes the opposite of friendly. It is derived from the Latin *bellum*, "war." This root, too, is shared by several other words. A *belligerent* person is one who is aggressive and eager to fight. *Belligerents* are the countries engaged in fighting a war. The *antebellum* period refers particularly to the time before the American Civil War, especially as it relates to the South. A *casus belli* is a term in international law for an act that provokes or is used to justify a war.

Review for Lessons 9–12

Crossword Puzzle Solve the crossword puzzle below by studying the clues and filling in the answer boxes. Clues followed by a number are definitions of words in Lessons 9 through 12. The number gives the word list in which the answer to the clue appears.

Clues Across

1. A coming or arrival (9)

6. The point opposite the base (10)

9. A nickname (12)

10. To attack as false (12)

11. Twain's *The Adventures of Tom* _____

13. Fresh and juicy (11)

14. Peaceful relations; friendship (12)

17. To invent in order to deceive (9)

19. Not expensive

20. Activity for which one is well suited (12)

23. Flat, treeless plains of the arctic (11)

26. Opposite of *north*

27. Indifferent or uninterested (9)

28. Plant from which oil is extracted

29. A sudden collapse or downfall (10)

31. An ample amount (11)

32. Equivalent to; the same as (12)

Clues Down

2. One's place of residence (9)

3. One who rides on horseback (10)

4. A thing assumed to be self-evident (11)

5. Green with vegetation (10)

7. To raise in rank, wealth, or honor (12)

8. The Garden of _____

12. The exact opposite (12)

15. To settle, calm, or satisfy (10)

16. Suffering from extreme poverty (12)

18. To obliterate completely (10)

21. Having to do with the countryside

22. A strong, irrational fear (9)

24. Opposite of 21 down

25. Main attraction at a circus

30. Short for Central Intelligence Agency

Lesson 13

Word List
Study the definitions of the words below; then do the exercises for the lesson.

altruism
al´ trōō iz əm

n. The putting of others' well-being ahead of one's own; unselfishness.
The Salvation Army's **altruism** is often expressed at holiday times through gifts of food for those who have little.
altruistic *adj.*
As children mature, they become more **altruistic** and less self-centered.

concurrent
kən kʉr´ ənt

adj. Taking place at the same time; simultaneous.
Moving from table to table as the games progressed, the chessmaster played sixteen **concurrent** games and won them all.

context
kän´ tekst

n. 1. The circumstances in which something exists or occurs.
We can better understand Dale's inflammatory statements if we consider the **context** in which they were made.
2. The surroundings of a word or phrase in a spoken or written passage.
The meaning of words like "draw" can often be determined only by examining the **context** in which they occur.

crass
kras

adj. Lacking delicacy or sensitivity; gross.
Molly's **crass** suggestion that I baby-sit for her on Saturday nights since I never seem to have a date hurt me.

cuisine
kwi zēn´

n. Style of cooking.
Indian **cuisine** uses a savory array of spices.

debase
dē bās´

v. To lower the quality, character, or status of; to devalue.
The Watergate conspiracy did much to **debase** the American presidency.

enjoin
en join´

v. 1. To direct or command.
The judge **enjoined** the jury to refrain from discussing the controversial case.
2. To forbid or prohibit.
The rules **enjoin** smoking on school property.

extemporaneous
ek stem pə rā´ nē əs

adj. Composed or performed on the spur of the moment, with little or no planning.
Public figures need to master the art of **extemporaneous** speaking, since they often need to improvise before an audience.

genesis
jen´ ə sis

n. An origin, creation, or beginning.
Naomi's visit to Kuwait was the **genesis** of her interest in Islam.

libation
lī bā´ shən

n. A liquid, especially when poured as an offering or drunk as part of a ceremony.
The celebrants poured out their cups as a **libation** to the harvest god.

malaise
ma lāz´

n. A vague feeling of uneasiness or unwellness.
My headache and general **malaise** turned out to be incipient flu symptoms.

| **platitude** | *n.* A thought or remark that is dull or trite. |
| plat´ ə tōōd | It was refreshing to hear the candidate for governor offer fresh ideas instead of **platitudes**. |

reconcile	*v.* 1. To reestablish an amicable relationship.
rek´ ən sīl	Family members tried to **reconcile** the feuding brothers.
	2. To bring to quiet submission.
	I **reconciled** myself to the inevitability of not getting a summer job.
	3. To bring into harmony or agreement.
	It's difficult for us to **reconcile** your account of the graduation party with events as we experienced them.

| **sunder** | *v.* To break or force apart; to sever. |
| sun´ dər | A bolt of lightning **sundered** the rock neatly down the middle. |

travail	*n.* 1. Activity that is arduous and burdensome; toil.
trə vāl´	The difficult expedition to reach the source of the Irrawaddy was a six-month **travail**.
	2. Suffering or anguish.
	The **travail** inflicted by the Civil War left the nation eager to heal its divisions.

13A Understanding Meanings

Read the sentences below. If a sentence correctly uses the word in bold, write *C* on the line below it. If a sentence is incorrect, rewrite it so that the vocabulary word in bold is used correctly.

1. The **genesis** of a project is the way it came into being.

_____

2. To **reconcile** people to a situation is to cause them to accept it.

_____

3. **Cuisine** is knowledge of how to behave in social situations.

_____

4. **Crass** behavior reflects empathy with others' feelings.

_____

5. An action that is **enjoined** is demanded by one in authority.

_____

6. **Altruism** is an unselfish concern for the welfare of others.

_____

7. A **libation** is a feast to celebrate an anniversary or similar event.

8. **Travail** is difficult and often painful activity.

9. **Concurrent** events happen one after the other in quick succession.

10. **Malaise** is a general feeling of mental or physical discomfort.

11. **Platitudes** are statements offered to encourage.

12. To **debase** a currency is to lower its value.

13. **Extemporaneous** remarks are those that are carefully rehearsed.

14. The **context** of a sentence is the passages that precede and follow it.

altruism

concurrent

context

crass

cuisine

debase

enjoin

extemporaneous

genesis

libation

malaise

platitude

reconcile

sunder

travail

15. To **sunder** a relationship is to cut it off.

13B Using Words

If the word (or a form of the word) in bold fits in a sentence in the group below it, write the word in the blank space. If the word does not fit, leave the space empty.

1. **debase**

   (a) Personal attacks on candidates _____ the level of political discourse.

   (b) Printing excessive amounts of paper money will _____ a nation's currency.

   (c) Giving inflated grades serves only to _____ the value of education.

2. **platitude**

   (a) Contributors received letters of thanks for their _____ to the society.

   (b) "You're as young as you feel" is a _____ I hear often from Uncle Bert.

   (c) New Hampshire license plates bear the _____ "Live Free Or Die."

3. **enjoin**

   (a) We _____ our hands and formed a circle and then stood in silence.

   (b) The appeals court _____ the union members to return to work.

   (c) The Catholic Church _____ the ordination of women as priests.

4. **concurrent**

   (a) Babylon's rise to military power was _____ with its rise to economic power.

   (b) Dwight D. Eisenhower served two _____ terms as president.

   (c) Two _____ four-year sentences mean no more than a four-year prison term.

5. **travail**

   (a) Crossing the Gobi desert in winter is a _____ even for experienced trekkers.

   (b) In the lunar rover, astronauts were able to _____ the surface of the moon.

   (c) He wrote a book detailing his six-year _____ as a prisoner in Vietnam.

6. **context**

   (a) A word's meaning becomes clearer if you look at the _____ of the sentence.

   (b) The author provides the _____ in which the events of the 1960s occurred.

   (c) We planted the flowering cherry tree within the _____ of the patio.

7. **reconcile**

   (a) After a six-month trial separation, June and Galen agreed to _____ .

   (b) I'm trying to _____ these payments with the amounts listed in my checkbook.

   (c) Monks must _____ themselves to a life of poverty.

8. **sunder**

   (a) An explosive charge was used to _____ the rock.

   (b) Junius and Terry vowed that nothing would be allowed to _____ their friendship.

   (c) Enormous energy is required to _____ the nucleus of an atom.

13C Word Study

Fill in the missing word in each of the sentences below. Then write a brief definition of the word. The number in parentheses gives the lesson from which the word is taken.

1. The prefix *ad-* means "towards." It combines with the Latin *venire* (to come) to form the English word _____ (9), meaning

   _____ .

2. The prefix *pro-* means "before." It combines with the Latin *clivus* (slope) to form the English word _____ (9), meaning

   _____ .

3. The Latin *itinerari* (to travel) forms the English word _____ (9), meaning

   _____ .

4. The prefix *ob-* means "against." It combines with the Latin *probrum* (reproach) to form the English word _____ (10), meaning

   _____ .

5. The prefix *un-* means "not." It combines with the prefix *equi-* (equal) and the Latin *voc* (voice) to form the English word _____ (11), meaning

   _____ .

6. The Latin *domus* (home) forms the English word _____ (9), meaning

   _____ .

7. The prefix *anti-* means "against." It combines with the Greek *tithenai* (to set) to form the English word _____ (12), meaning

   _____ .

8. The prefix *ad-* means "towards." It combines with the Latin *terere* (to rub) to form the English word _____ (10), meaning

   _____ .

9. The prefix *re-* means "again." It combines with the Latin *conciliare* (to unite) to form the English word _____ (13), meaning

   _____ .

altruism

concurrent

context

crass

cuisine

debase

enjoin

extemporaneous

genesis

libation

malaise

platitude

reconcile

sunder

travail

10. The prefix *multi-* means "many." It combines with the Latin *fariam* (ways)

to form the English word _____ (11), meaning

_____ .

13D Images of Words

Circle the letter of each sentence that suggests the numbered bold vocabulary word. In each group, you may circle more than one letter or none at all.

1. **cuisine**

   (a) Mediterranean peoples often use garlic and olive oil when cooking.

   (b) For lunch I had a tuna sandwich with lettuce and tomato.

   (c) One of the inn's specialties is New England boiled beef dinner.

2. **extemporaneous**

   (a) The fire appears to have started from a bundle of oily rags left on the floor.

   (b) The best jazz occurs when the musicians feel free to improvise.

   (c) Melia's best witticisms are always made up on the spur of the moment.

3. **concurrent**

   (a) After the 2000 elections, the Republicans controlled both Congress and the White House.

   (b) The flower show is always held on the first day of spring.

   (c) Liz was asked to name the president and vice president now in office.

4. **malaise**

   (a) The patient complained of vague aches and a general loss of energy.

   (b) The nation seemed aimless, without a sense of purpose after its defeat.

   (c) I told Helene it was time for her to stop brooding and get on with her life.

5. **travail**

   (a) Sarrenth and her family walked for days without food during their escape from Cambodia.

   (b) Scott and his party perished in a failed attempt to reach the South Pole.

   (c) Much is demanded from those to whom much is given.

6. **genesis**

   (a) The need to determine a ship's longitude led to the first chronometer.

   (b) I opened the book to page one and began reading.

   (c) The solar system was formed out of a cloud of interstellar matter.

7. **altruism**

   (a) We agreed not to spend more than $10 on each gift for family members.

   (b) Most blood donors give out of a desire to help someone in need.

   (c) We are told that it is better to give than to receive.

8. **crass**

   (a) The day of the accident, lawyers were calling Ms. West about suing the company.

   (b) Sam walked nervously over to Alyssa and asked her to go to the movies with him.

   (c) Cousin Charlie tried to sell insurance to the mourners at Grandpa's funeral.

9. **platitude**

   (a) Students are expected to make mistakes; that is how they learn.

   (b) "Ah, well," Robert said. "It takes all kinds to make a world."

   (c) I nodded when Adjowah assured me that money can't buy happiness.

10. **libation**

    (a) They accepted a glass of wine in honor of their fiftieth wedding anniversary.

    (b) Water may be substituted for wine during that ritual.

    (c) Tyler poured herself a glass of fresh, cold orange juice.

13E Passage

Read the passage below; then complete the exercise that follows it.

Kwanzaa

Beginning just ten years after Columbus's voyage of 1492 and continuing for the next 350 years, Africans were taken by force from their homelands and brought to the Americas as slaves. The slave traders and owners not only deprived Africans of their freedom but also stripped away their identity for when these men, women, and children were carried off in chains, ties to their home cultures were **sundered**. Africans in the New World struggled to maintain their customs and beliefs, in spite of the **travails** of slavery. Yet much was lost. They had to create a new cultural identity in the **context** of the nascent American society that had enslaved them.

In 1965, African American professor Maulana Karenga, keenly aware of this history, was deeply disturbed by the violent riots that had just taken place in Watts, a primarily black section of Los Angeles. The riots were born of frustration over injustices including poverty, unemployment, poor housing, and inadequate health care, and of a widespread lack of hope. Karenga believed that the **malaise** that afflicted many urban African Americans was caused not just by physical poverty but by spiritual and cultural deprivation as well. His resolve to address these issues was the **genesis** of a unique holiday that draws upon the rich cultural heritage of people of African ancestry.

"There is nothing so powerful as an idea whose time has come" may sound like a **platitude**, but it certainly applies to Karenga's idea. The holiday he proposed, to which he gave the name Kwanzaa, is today celebrated by millions of people, not only African Americans, but also people of African descent in countries around the world. The name comes from the Swahili phrase *matunda ya kwanza*, meaning "first fruits." It is celebrated **concurrently** with the Christmas–New Year holiday season, although it has no religious significance.

Karenga based Kwanzaa on "Nguzo Saba," seven principles, which he drew from African thought. The first is *Umoja (unity)*. African Americans are called upon to **reconcile** differences between one another and to strive for unity in family, community, nation, and race. Next is *Kujichagulia (self-determination)*. To be controlled by others is **debasing** to the human spirit; real power comes from defining, naming, creating, and speaking for oneself and one's people. *Ujima (collective work and responsibility)* fosters the spirit of **altruism** by encouraging individuals to take responsibility for the well-being of others and to solve problems and build community together.

altruism

concurrent

context

crass

cuisine

debase

enjoin

extemporaneous

genesis

libation

malaise

platitude

reconcile

sunder

travail

The next principle, *Ujamaa (cooperative economics)*, stresses the value of African American ownership of businesses and **enjoins** others in the community to support them. The fifth principle is *Nia (purpose)*. Its goal is to make the collective building of strong communities the vocation of African American people. *Kuumba (creativity)* stresses the importance of seeking new and personal ways for individuals to leave their communities more beautiful and beneficial than they were before. The final principle, *Imani (faith)*, stresses the cultivation of a strong belief in the African American people, in parents and leaders, and in the rightness and victory of their struggle.

African Americans celebrate Kwanzaa by laying out a woven mat, on which they place fruits and vegetables symbolizing the rewards of collective labor and ears of corn representing the children. These items reflect the traditions of the African harvest celebrations that Kwanzaa stems from. A candelabra, called a *kinara*, holds seven candles: a black one in the center, three red ones to the left, and three green ones to the right. The three colors represent the people, their struggle, and the future and hope, respectively. The individual candles represent the Nguzo Saba, the seven principles that are the foundation of the holiday. The black candle is lit on the first day of Kwanzaa, and another on each of the following six days, alternating from left to right. After the candle is lit, those present discuss the principle of the day and how they strive to embody it in daily life.

On the evening of the sixth day, usually December 31, a feast called the *Karamu* is held. Participants bring dishes that represent the best of African American **cuisine**. At the feast, a cup is filled and **libations** are offered. Then the cup is passed around to all present to take a sip. After the feast, the celebrants, beginning with the eldest, speak **extemporaneously** about their life experiences, their pleasure at being present, and their hopes for the future. On the last day, presents may be exchanged, but the **crass** giving of overly expensive store-bought gifts is discouraged. Instead, books and handmade gifts reflecting African heritage are preferred.

Answer each of the following questions in the form of a sentence. If a question does not contain a vocabulary word from this lesson's word list, use one in your answer. Use each word only once.

1. What was the **context** in which the idea for Kwanzaa came about?

2. If you were at a Kwanzaa meal, would you enjoy the **extemporaneous** speeches? Explain your answer.

3. According to the passage, what are some of the long-term effects for the descendants of the African people who were **sundered** from their cultures?

4. What kind of **reconciliation** does the festival of Kwanzaa encourage?

5. In what way, do you think, would the giving of very expensive gifts **debase** the principles of Kwanzaa?

6. Describe the role of food and drink in the Kwanzaa celebration.

7. Do you think it is accurate to describe the seven principles of Kwanzaa as **platitudes**? Explain your answer.

8. In what way might following the principles of Kwanzaa alleviate some of the **travails** of people's lives?

9. How is **altruism** encouraged by the principles of Kwanzaa?

10. Would it be accurate to say that the lighting of the black candle is **concurrent** with the feast of *karamu*? Explain your answer.

FUN & FASCINATING FACTS

Most people regard travel as pleasurable, except perhaps those who must do it constantly in the course of their work. It's curious, therefore, that **travail** and *travel* once meant the same thing. This fact is a reminder that there was a time when travel was always slow, often uncomfortable, and sometimes dangerous. The etymology of *travail* vividly reinforces its modern associations with painful activity. It comes from the Latin *trepalium*, a three-staked Roman instrument used for torture.

Lesson 14

Word List
Study the definitions of the words below; then do the exercises for the lesson.

abeyance
ə bā´ əns

n. A state of (usually temporary) inactivity or suspension.
Construction of the new city hall was in **abeyance** while the city council sought additional funds.

buttress
bu´ trəs

n. 1. A projecting structure that supports a wall or building.
The wall would have collapsed without the stone **buttresses** protruding from it.
2. Anything that supports or protects.
Freedom of the press is a **buttress** against tyranny.
v. To support or strengthen.
Mr. Orantes **buttressed** his lawsuit with photographs of the accident.

commensurate
kə men´ sə rət

adj. Corresponding in size, degree, or amount; proportionate; of equal value.
The students were put in groups **commensurate** with their reading abilities.

dilatory
dil´ ə tôr ē

adj. Slow to act or respond; delaying, tardy.
The phone company discontinues service to customers who are **dilatory** in paying their bills.

ecumenical
ek´ yo͞o men´ i kəl

adj. Universal; inclusive, especially concerning religious matters.
The **ecumenical** council promotes cooperation among multifarious groups of churches.

facade
fə säd´

(also, façade) *n.* 1. The front or face of a building.
The building was shingled except for its brick **facade** which faced the street.
2. A superficial appearance; an illusion.
Connie's pleasant demeanor was a **facade** for the anger she felt.

gargoyle
gär´ goil

n. A grotesque stone figure used as a decorative feature on a building or as an ornament; a spout projecting.
The stone faces of **gargoyles** projecting beyond the roof line acted as rain spouts.

moot
mo͞ot

v. To debate, suggest, or discuss.
The issue of changing the dress code is often **mooted** but never resolved.
adj. Deprived of significance; irrelevant.
We're moving at the end of the month, so the possibility of a rent increase is **moot**.

pinnacle
pin´ ə kəl

n. 1. A tall, slender, pointed top; peak.
The icicles hung from the roof like inverted **pinnacles**.
2. The highest point of achievement.
The **pinnacle** of Wilma Rudolph's sports career was competing in the Olympics.

requiem
rek´ wē əm

n. A funeral mass or service; a musical composition honoring the dead.
The **requiem** for the late president was carried live on television.

sacrosanct
sak´ rō saŋkt

adj. Highly sacred or holy; not to be violated.
The concepts of yin and yang are **sacrosanct** to Taoist believers.

sensuous
sen´ shōo əs

adj. 1. Coming from or acting on the senses.
The **sensuous** curves of the new museum's exterior are a delight to the eye.
2. Producing an agreeable effect on the senses.
The cat stretched out in front of the fire in **sensuous** contentment.

tenet
ten´ ət

n. A principle or belief held to be true, especially by members of an organization.
One of the academy's traditional **tenets** was that behavioral standards would be maintained through an honor code.

transcend
tran send´

v. To go above the limits of; to exceed or surpass.
The need for emergency aid to the refugees allowed Congress to **transcend** partisan disagreement.

venue
ven´ yōo

n. The scene or locale of any action or event; the place of an alleged crime.
The **venue** for the jazz festival has yet to be determined, but several sites are under consideration.

14A Understanding Meanings

Read the sentences below. If a sentence correctly uses the word in bold, write *C* on the line below it. If a sentence is incorrect, rewrite it so that the vocabulary word in bold is used correctly.

1. A **facade** is a false appearance intended to deceive.

2. A **venue** is a route or path to be followed.

3. To be **commensurate** with something is to be in proportion to it.

abeyance
buttress
commensurate
dilatory
ecumencial
facade
gargoyle
moot
pinnacle
requiem
sacrosanct
sensuous
tenet
transcend
venue

4. A **gargoyle** is a liquid used to rinse the throat.

5. To **buttress** a proposal is to undermine it.

6. A **requiem** is the swearing-in ceremony of a national leader.

7. **Sensuous** elements are those that have a pleasing effect on the senses.

8. To **transcend** something is to go above or beyond it.

_____

9. An **ecumenical** council examines the financial records of diverse groups.

_____

10. When something is in **abeyance**, it is halted for a time.

_____

11. A **pinnacle** is a spire on the top of a building.

_____

12. A **tenet** is one who has signed a lease to occupy a building.

_____

13. To **moot** a topic is to bring it up for discussion.

_____

14. A **dilatory** response is one that is very carefully thought out.

_____

15. A **sacrosanct** rule is one that is inviolable.

_____

14B Using Words

If the word (or a form of the word) in bold fits a sentence in the group below it, write the word in the blank. If the word does not fit, leave the space empty.

1. **moot**

   (a) The debate over summer camps became _____ when Brett accepted a job offer instead.

   (b) Jerome _____ that the family buy a new car, but his parents overruled him.

   (c) The health-care proposal was _____ a year ago but was never seriously considered.

2. **sensuous**

   (a) Those entering paradise were promised an eternity of _____ delights.

   (b) Many of Keats's poems possess a _____ beauty that lingers in the mind.

   (c) I was _____ of the need to protect myself against possible danger.

3. **ecumenical**

   (a) The _____ movement seeks to unite Protestants and Roman Catholics.

   (b) The United Nations is an _____ organization of almost 200 nations.

   (c) These _____ tools have an astonishing range of industrial applications.

4. **sacrosanct**

   (a) Because places of worship were considered _____ , they were left unharmed during the war.

   (b) The Republicans said no program was _____ when the budget required cuts.

   (c) The _____ mouse avoided the trap we set out.

5. **abeyance**

   (a) Backstage problems caused a slight _____ in raising the curtain.

   (b) Many laws had fallen into _____ and were no longer being enforced.

   (c) Construction was held in _____ until the builders obtained the necessary permits.

6. **dilatory**

   (a) The Smythes were quick to incur debts, but _____ in repaying them.

   (b) The lawyers' _____ tactics succeeded in prolonging the case unnecessarily.

   (c) My cat's pupils are _____ when she needs to see in the dark.

7. **commensurate**

   (a) We know that Rachel's recent grades are not _____ with her abilities.

   (b) At the _____ ceremonies, 300 students were awarded master's degrees.

   (c) The one-bedroom apartment was _____ with the needs of the young couple.

8. **gargoyle**

   (a) The villain in the play looked like a _____ and repulsed everyone in the audience.

   (b) A _____ of flowers and braided vines was hung over the doorway.

   (c) The _____ had a grotesque human head and a goat's body.

abeyance
buttress
commensurate
dilatory
ecumenical
facade
gargoyle
moot
pinnacle
requiem
sacrosanct
sensuous
tenet
transcend
venue

14C Word Study

Each group of four words below contains two words that are either synonyms or antonyms. Circle these two words, then circle the S if they are synonyms, the A if they are antonyms.

1. commensurate	dilatory	itinerant	prompt	S	A
2. requiem	platitude	belief	tenet	S	A
3. libation	origin	genesis	context	S	A
4. unite	sunder	enjoin	relegate	S	A
5. penurious	craven	salubrious	affluent	S	A
6. plenitude	sobriquet	amity	friendship	S	A
7. prodigious	pugnacious	bellicose	avuncular	S	A
8. multifarious	ambiguous	itinerant	unequivocal	S	A
9. wholesome	salubrious	recondite	inveterate	S	A
10. disinter	postulate	divest	bury	S	A

14D Images of Words

Circle the letter of each sentence that suggests the numbered bold vocabulary word. In each group, you may circle more than one letter or none at all.

1. **dilatory**

   (a) As it gets darker, the pupils of the eyes grow larger to let in more light.

   (b) Having waited until the last minute to call the theater box office, Tracy found there were no tickets left.

   (c) The night before the paper was due, Stephen still had not written a word.

2. **moot**

   (a) Beryl couldn't decide whether to get a golden retriever or a Labrador.

   (b) While the children argued over the last popsicle, it melted.

   (c) The proposal for a new bridge came up at today's city council meeting.

3. **requiem**

   (a) All first- and second-year students are required to take physical education.

   (b) A mass for the deceased bishop was held in St. Patrick's Cathedral.

   (c) Mozart and Verdi both wrote solemn music suitable for funerals.

4. **tenet**

   (a) Scientific experiments should be conducted several times to confirm their results.

   (b) In the game of chess, the player with the white pieces usually moves first.

   (c) You cannot be a Muslim unless you accept Muhammad as the true prophet.

5. **venue**

   (a) Lawyers for the accused wanted the trial moved out of Oklahoma City.

   (b) The 2002 Winter Olympics were held in Salt Lake City, Utah.

   (c) The White House is located at 1600 Pennsylvania Avenue in Washington, D.C.

6. **sacrosanct**

   (a) This part of the church is off limits to tourists and other casual visitors.

   (b) Athena, the Greek goddess of wisdom, may have originated in Crete.

   (c) Pacifists believe that the value of human life is sacred.

7. **pinnacle**

   (a) When she won an Academy Award, the actress felt she'd reached the highest point in her career.

   (b) Atop the castle's tallest spire a flag fluttered in the breeze.

   (c) The base of the Great Pyramid covers an area of thirteen acres.

8. **transcend**

   (a) In 1903, Fanny Workman set an altitude record for women by climbing Mt. Lungma, with a height of 22,568 feet.

   (b) Multinational corporations have interests beyond the border of a single country.

   (c) The author's vision goes beyond space and time to unknown realms.

9. **facade**

   (a) Each surface of the diamond is cut so as to reflect light.

   (b) What seemed to be a storefront was a painted wall supported from behind.

   (c) The great and powerful Wizard of Oz was really a man hiding behind a curtain.

10. **buttress**

   (a) Without this support, the weight of the building would push out the wall.

   (b) Shirley's habit of interrupting our conversations became annoying.

   (c) Lawyers often cite previous cases to strengthen their arguments.

abeyance
buttress
commensurate
dilatory
ecumencial
facade
gargoyle
moot
pinnacle
requiem
sacrosanct
sensuous
tenet
transcend
venue

14E Passage

Read the passage below; then complete the exercise that follows it.

Washington National Cathedral

When delegates from Israel and several Arab states arrived in the United States for Middle East peace talks in late 1991, it seemed appropriate that they, together with their American hosts, should participate in an **ecumenical** religious service. As it happened, an appropriate **venue** for such a gathering, Washington National Cathedral, had been completed just one year before. There, under its great, vaulted 120-foot ceiling, followers of the Christian, Muslim, and Jewish faiths were able to **transcend** their differences temporarily and join in an act of worship.

When the nation's capital was being laid out, the idea for a national cathedral was **mooted** by French architect Pierre L'Enfant, who was selected by George Washington to draw up a plan. L'Enfant proposed "a great church for national purposes . . . equally open to all," but the idea fell into **abeyance** because of concern that such an institution would violate a major **tenet** of the constitution forbidding the establishment of a state-approved religion.

It was not until 1893, exactly one hundred years after Washington had laid the cornerstone of the Capitol building, that Congress granted a charter to the Protestant Episcopal Cathedral Foundation to build what is variously known as Washington National Cathedral and the National Cathedral, but whose official name is the Cathedral Church of Saint Peter and Saint Paul. Because no government money was to be used to build this edifice, the **sacrosanct** separation of church and state would be preserved. The cathedral was to have no local congregation, serving instead as an interreligious house of worship for the entire nation.

Fifty-seven acres on Mount St. Alban, the highest point in the city, were chosen as the site. President Theodore Roosevelt laid the cornerstone for the new building in 1907 before a crowd of ten thousand or more onlookers. Work proceeded at a pace **commensurate** with the magnitude of the project. Eighty-three years passed before the final piece of stone was set in place to complete the **pinnacle** on the South Tower of what became the sixth-largest cathedral in the world. If this time span suggests a **dilatory** pace, consider this: England's Canterbury Cathedral took five hundred years to complete!

The cathedral was built in the fourteenth-century English Gothic style: **buttresses** supported the exterior walls and **gargoyles** looked out over the city. Dozens of sculptors, stone masons, and artists working in stained glass, metal, and needlepoint devoted countless hours to its embellishment. One of the cathedral's more than 200 stained glass windows even commemorates the 1969 lunar landing, and embedded in one of the windows is a sliver of moon rock that was presented by the Apollo 11 crew.

On the west **facade** of the cathedral, the space above one of the doors is adorned with an elaborate sculptural relief twenty-one feet across entitled *The Creation*, originally called *Ex Nihilo* ("Out of Nothing"). It is a **sensuous** composition of male and female figures emerging from the void. The artist was Frederick Hart, who also sculpted the seven-foot bronze statute *The Three Servicemen* that faces Washington's Vietnam Veterans Memorial.

Although the National Cathedral is still in its infancy, especially when compared with the venerable Gothic cathedrals of Europe, it has already begun to gather historical associations. The **requiem** service for President Eisenhower was held there in 1969. By her own request, Helen Keller, together with her former teacher and lifelong companion Anne Sullivan, is buried there, as are President and Mrs. Woodrow Wilson. And the last Sunday sermon that Dr. Martin Luther King, Jr. preached before his tragic assassination in Memphis, Tennessee, was delivered from its pulpit.

Answer each of the following questions in the form of a sentence. If a question does not contain a vocabulary word from this lesson's word list, use one in your answer. Use each word only once.

1. Why is the absence of a state religion considered **sacrosanct** in America?

2. Would it be accurate to describe L'Enfant's idea for a national church as **ecumenical**? Explain your answer.

3. Why was Washington, D.C., chosen as the site of the cathedral?

4. How was Congress **dilatory** in granting its charter?

5. What **tenets** of gothic architecture were followed in constructing the cathedral?

6. Was use of the building held in **abeyance** until it was completed? Explain your answer.

7. How is it suggested that the Frederick Hart relief consists of gentle curves rather than jagged lines?

8. What details suggest that Washington Cathedral is **commensurate** in size with cathedrals in other parts of the world?

9. How does the Episcopalian Church **transcend** its own religious point of view in running the cathedral?

10. Why is it likely that the **pinnacles** of Washington Cathedral's towers are visible from a distance?

In Old French, the language of France from the ninth to the early sixteenth centuries, the word *gargoule* meant both "throat" and "water spout." The word probably originated in imitation of the sound of swallowed liquid going down the throat and of water passing through a spout. Medieval stone carvers gave the fantastic shapes of grotesque creatures to spouts designed to carry rainwater clear of the roof. The name **gargoyle** came to be applied to these creations or to anything resembling them. The etymology of *gargle* can be traced to the same Old French source. We gargle by holding liquid in the throat while exhaling air through it.

A **pinnacle** is a slender, pointed ornamental feature that sits atop a structure much like a feather is a decorative addition to a hat. The comparison is apt because the word is derived from the Latin *pinna* or *penna*, "a feather." Another word sharing this root is pen. Pens were once made of feathers with the quill split at the end to hold ink.

Lesson 15

Word List
Study the definitions of the words below; then do the exercises for the lesson.

arbiter
är´ bi tər

n. One whose decisions are accepted as final; a judge.
Unable to agree, management and labor appointed an **arbiter** to resolve their conflict.

conclave
kän´ klāv

n. A private meeting or secret assembly.
With the paper's deadline approaching, the **conclave** of editors and reporters trying to decide whether or not to run the news story had not yet adjourned.

concomitant
kən käm´ i tənt

adj. Accompanying; occupying or existing at the same time.
The popularity of the World Wide Web, and the **concomitant** increase in computer sales, has been a boon to software and computer manufacturers.

coterie
kō´ tər ē

n. An intimate or exclusive group; a clique.
Several members of the hockey team became a **coterie** that ate together every day.

demur
də myōor´

v. To raise objections; to withhold one's approval or agreement.
While Eleanor supported Ms. Villatoro for the director's position, Sebastian **demurred**, arguing that she lacked experience.

entice
en tīs´

v. To lead or persuade by arousing desire or hope; allure.
The beautiful holiday window display was meant to **entice** customers into the department store.
enticing *adj.*
The **enticing** aroma of Dad's famous pecan pie drew me to the kitchen.

flaunt
flônt

v. To parade or display conspicuously or boldly.
Joe **flaunted** his new knowledge of French by sprinkling his conversations with French phrases.

genteel
jen tēl´

adj. Polite, elegant, stylish; sometimes overly so.
Tomas's **genteel** manner was especially noticeable when contrasted with the behavior of his raucous friends.

graphic
graf´ ik

adj. 1. Evoking a sharp mental picture; vivid.
Viviana described the forest in such **graphic** detail that I could almost feel the leaves crunch under my feet.
2. Concerning the pictorial arts, as drawing, painting, etc.
My art teacher says that watercolor is the most challenging medium in the **graphic** arts.

inimical
in im´ i kəl

adj. 1. Expressing hostility or unfriendly intent.
Bella's **inimical** stare suggested that a conflict might be brewing.
2. Having adverse or harmful effects.
It has been proven beyond any doubt that excessive use of alcohol is **inimical** to one's health.

inordinate
in ôr´ də nət

adj. Beyond what is ordinary or reasonable in amount or scope; excessive.
The summer school report required several days of study due to its **inordinate** length.

ludicrous loo´ di krəs	*adj.* Provoking or describing laughter because of absurdity; ridiculous. Dmitri could not keep a straight face when he put on the **ludicrous** feather costume provided him for the school play.
oligarchy äl´ i gär kē	*n.* Government by a small, elite group. Haiti was an **oligarchy** in which a few wealthy families controlled the country's military, political, and economic affairs.
redoubtable ri dou´ tə bəl	*adj.* Worthy of respect; formidable. I was relieved when I learned that the **redoubtable** lawyer, admired by all, was on my side.
repugnant rē pug´ nənt	*adj.* Highly distasteful; offensive; repulsive. The candidate's divisive rhetoric was **repugnant** to voters of all races, and he finished last in the election.

15A Understanding Meanings

Read the sentences below. If a sentence correctly uses the word in bold, write *C* on the line below it. If a sentence is incorrect, rewrite it so that the vocabulary word in bold is used correctly.

1. A **genteel** person has refined manners.

_____

2. A **graphic** description is one that makes a strikingly clear impression.

_____

3. Events that are **concomitant** are of equal importance.

_____

4. To **flaunt** one's knowledge is to make a big show of it.

_____

5. An **oligarchy** is a multiparty political system.

_____

6. To **entice** someone is to hold them spellbound.

_____

7. An **inimical** gaze is one that communicates animosity.

_____

8. An **inordinate** amount is one that cannot be measured.

9. A **ludicrous** statement is one that is laughable for its foolishness.

10. A **coterie** is a small, select group.

11. A **repugnant** suggestion is one that has only lackluster support.

12. To **demur** is to decline to give one's approval.

13. A **conclave** is the meeting of a group assembled for a special purpose.

14. A **redoubtable** scholar is one whose credentials are questionable.

15. An **arbiter** is a person who vacillates when called upon to decide.

arbiter
conclave
concomitant
coterie
demur
entice
flaunt
genteel
graphic
inimical
inordinate
ludicrous
oligarchy
redoubtable
repugnant

15B Using Words

If the word (or a form of the word) in bold fits in a sentence in the group below it, write the word in the blank space. If the word does not fit, leave the space empty.

1. **repugnant**

(a) The committee chair was _____ to the proposal of relaxing handgun control.

(b) Jolene declared that unlike some people she doesn't find bats _____ .

(c) The exploitation of child workers in other parts of the world is _____ .

2. **inordinate**

(a) He's a fairly _____ person who keeps to himself and never bothers anyone.

(b) The mayor's _____ desire for public approval makes it difficult for him to govern.

(c) Rufino ate an _____ number of fried clams and later paid the price.

3. **demur**

   (a) I hope Mara will not _____ when I propose her as a Science Society member.

   (b) I hesitate to _____ when so many favor the plan, but I'm afraid I must.

   (c) When the region of Biafra tried to _____ from Nigeria, civil war erupted.

4. **entice**

   (a) Keith left out an open can of tuna to _____ his cat from hiding.

   (b) Cedric decided he would _____ Keiko to his birthday party.

   (c) A celebrity endorsement can _____ Elaine to long for almost any product.

5. **redoubtable**

   (a) In the state final, the Wolverines challenged the _____ Panthers.

   (b) It was growing increasingly _____ that my money would ever be returned.

   (c) The sunset over the Pacific was a truly _____ sight.

6. **inimical**

   (a) If both parties are _____ to the proposed settlement, it will be dropped.

   (b) We don't want you to do anything _____ to your interests.

   (c) Policies beneficial to health-care providers may be _____ to patients.

7. **flaunt**

   (a) Alex _____ his vocabulary by using words no one had ever heard of.

   (b) Frank _____ his newly acquired wealth by giving $100 tips to doormen.

   (c) Shannon _____ her friendship ring by gesturing conspicuously with her hand.

8. **graphic**

   (a) There was a _____ description of the coup attempt in today's *Times*.

   (b) Ms. Nesbit's critical articles concerned both the literary and the _____ arts.

   (c) The violence in that movie was so _____ that I couldn't watch it.

15C Word Study

Complete the analogies by selecting the pair of words whose relationship most resembles the relationship of the pair in capital letters. Circle the letter in front of the pair you choose.

1. PRAISE : EXALT ::
   (a) succumb : prevail   (c) interpose : interfere
   (b) scold : upbraid   (d) relegate : promote

2. CRAVEN : COURAGE ::
   (a) prodigious : size   (c) succulent : fruit
   (b) lazy : zeal   (d) multifarious : variety

3. ALTRUISM : GENEROSITY ::
   (a) levity : stupidity   (c) probity : dishonesty
   (b) autonomy : dependence   (d) privation : suffering

4. PLATITUDE : ORIGINALITY ::
   (a) regimen : exercise   (c) martinet : discipline
   (b) subterfuge : transparency   (d) epigram : brevity

5. RECONCILE : DIFFERENCES ::
   (a) accrue : interest   (c) fabricate : models
   (b) flaunt : numbers   (d) mediate : conflicts

6. FACADE : EDIFICE ::
   (a) face : head   (c) window : view
   (b) hand : glove   (d) fauna : plant

7. BUTTRESS : SUPPORT ::
   (a) subterfuge : deceive   (c) oxymoron : appease
   (b) philistine : demur   (d) libation : careen

8. VENUE : LOCATION
   (a) pinnacle : base   (c) proviso : condition
   (b) city : environs   (d) word : etymology

9. LUDICROUS : LAUGHTER
   (a) phlegmatic : malaise   (c) equestrian : horse
   (b) heinous : horror   (d) prodigious : size

10. DILATORY : SPEED ::
    (a) lilliputian : size   (c) succulent : conclave
    (b) apocryphal : doubt   (d) multifarious : variety

arbiter
conclave
concomitant
coterie
demur
entice
flaunt
genteel
graphic
inimical
inordinate
ludicrous
oligarchy
redoubtable
repugnant

15D Images of Words

Circle the letter of each sentence that suggests the numbered bold vocabulary word. In each group, you may circle more than one letter or none at all.

1. **coterie**

   (a) Travelers crossed the desert in groups in order to help each other survive.

   (b) This group of Wall Street traders behaves like an exclusive club.

   (c) Joan and her circle of friends keep separate from the class.

2. **genteel**

   (a) Sonia picked up the limping puppy, careful not to cause it further injury.

   (b) Grandfather thought it rude to use anything other than linen napkins.

   (c) It pained Aunt Sarah when we used expressions like "ain't" and "yeah."

3. **conclave**

   (a) Party leaders met in secret to choose a candidate for the presidency.

   (b) I met Rosie in the park today for a nice long chat.

   (c) The telescope's mirror curves like the inside of a bowl.

4. **arbiter**

   (a) I considered strawberry and chocolate, but finally chose the vanilla.

   (b) The Supreme Court has the final word on legal disputes.

   (c) Parents should be the judge of what is in their child's best interest.

5. **graphic**

   (a) Reading her account of the sailboat race was almost like being there.

   (b) With no public health services in place, the disease spread rapidly.

   (c) She took a stick and drew a line in the sand to separate the two teams.

6. **oligarchy**

   (a) Pol Pot exercised total power over the people of Cambodia.

   (b) United States cabinet members serve directly under the president.

   (c) Pakistan's "twenty-two families" were the actual rulers of the country.

7. **flaunt**

   (a) Despite the 30 mph speed limit, drivers on that part of Route 2 regularly go 50 to 60 mph.

   (b) Dave made a point of singing loudly when he was sure others would hear him.

   (c) The bodybuilders struck poses to show off their bulging muscles.

8. **concomitant**

   (a) Icy road conditions mean more auto accidents than usual.

   (b) Global warming is caused by increased carbon dioxide in the atmosphere.

   (c) If the supply of cod diminishes, then its price will certainly rise.

9. **demur**

   (a) Since Mrs. Martin is the expert, I'll let her answer your questions.

   (b) "I cannot accept your kind invitation to dinner tonight," said Alicia.

   (c) Anthony was too full to eat a second helping of dessert.

10. **ludicrous**

   (a) Mr. Piffle claims to have been Attila the Hun, Mahatma Gandhi, and Elvis Presley in previous lives.

   (b) We all laughed hysterically at the comic's routine about odd personal habits.

   (c) Based on what we now know, the idea of little green men from Mars is preposterous.

15E Passage

Read the passage below; then complete the exercise that follows it.

Birds of a Feather

The late nineteenth century in America is sometimes called the "Age of Elegance" because of the way its most privileged citizens **flaunted** their status by purchasing the most beautiful and elaborate homes, clothing, art, and other luxuries that money could buy. Women of this society competed with one another to display their beauty, refinement, and culture. As a result, they spent an **inordinate** amount of time on personal appearance, a preoccupation that was conspicuously apparent in the hats they wore.

In their efforts to produce ever more striking creations, hat designers made extravagant use of birds. They employed birds' feathers, wings, heads, as well as entire birds, and sometimes as many as six small birds on one hat. All kinds of birds were used including robins, scarlet tanagers, blue jays, woodpeckers, an owl, and different kinds of shore birds. An artistic arrangement of white egret plumes, known as aigrettes, atop a woman's head was believed to give her an **enticing** air. She might also glance demurely from behind a fan of dyed ostrich feathers. There was nothing new in this, of course. Feathers as articles of adornment or symbols of power had been prized for thousands of years, but during America's "Gilded Age," as this period is also known, things were getting out of hand. Five million birds were being killed annually in the United States to meet the demands of fashion.

Harriet Lawrence Hemenway was born into the **genteel** world of Boston high society in 1858. Her parents and grandparents were successful merchants and public benefactors, and she married into a family whose wealth equaled that of her own. Her position in society, reinforced by her strong personality, provided her with a **coterie** of admirers who welcomed her guidance in matters of fashion when they came together for afternoon teas, drawing room social gatherings, or grand balls. Exquisite clothing and elaborate aigrettes were very much a part of this exclusive world.

Change was in the air, however. Articles began appearing that described the cost of feathers: whole colonies of dead birds lying with their backs raw and bloody where plumes had been torn away, while their starving babies called piteously from their nests for food. Most of the young soon died. In 1895, Hemenway read an account of the slaughter of a heron colony. The **graphic** description made the use of feathers for personal embellishment **repugnant** to her. She banished them from her wardrobe and called upon her friends, who regarded her as an **arbiter** of fashion, to do the same. Women who **demurred** were excluded from social gatherings, which prompted many of them to change their minds. However, the boycott had little effect on the feather trade nationally. Hemenway carried the battle a stage further by organizing a **conclave** of the city's scientific and social elite to form the Massachusetts Audubon Society, modeled after the society formed in New York ten years earlier. Its stated purpose was "to discourage buying and wearing for ornamental purposes the feathers of any wild bird . . . and to otherwise further the protection of our native birds."

arbiter

conclave

concomitant

coterie

demur

entice

flaunt

genteel

graphic

inimical

inordinate

ludicrous

oligarchy

redoubtable

repugnant

Hemenway soon demonstrated that she was a **redoubtable** foe of the feather industry. Within a year, the society's membership approached the one thousand mark. Thick with names like Cabot, Lowell, Saltonstall, and Adams, it read like a roster of Boston's **oligarchy**. Over one hundred local chapters were established throughout the state, nearly all of them headed by women. By the turn of the century there were Audubon Societies in seventeen states, and in 1905 the National Association of Audubon Societies was formed.

A movement to ban the use of feathers for personal decoration was **inimical** to the interests of the feather industry. Companies fought back strenuously, arguing that ending the trade would cost many jobs. But the opposition remained adamant. In 1910, a bill passed in New York state prohibiting the sale of almost all North American nongame birds, either whole or parts. Then in 1913, Congress passed a bill to forbid the importation of any wild bird plumage. A senator from Missouri, arguing against it, made the **ludicrous** claim that God's purpose in creating herons had been "so that we could get aigrettes for the bonnets of our beautiful ladies." Further regulations to protect birds were enacted in later years.

The end of the trade in feathers and its **concomitant** reduction in the slaughter of birds was brought about by something more powerful than laws alone. The force of public opinion, led in Boston by Harriet Hemenway, had turned against it. Knowledge and determination had combined to start a movement for the protection of wildlife that thrives to this day.

Answer each of the following questions in the form of a sentence. If a question does not contain a vocabulary word from this lesson's word list, use one in your answer. Use each word only once.

1. Why do you think Harriet Hemenway and her friends and associates are described as Boston's **oligarchy**?

2. Why was Hemenway able to have a certain amount of influence with her friends?

3. In what way might a **genteel** upbringing have made Hemenway unlikely to question the source of her aigrettes?

4. Why was the article about how aigrettes were obtained effective in changing Hemenway's ideas about feather use?

5. How did the millinery industry **flaunt** their lack of interest in bird protection and conservation?

6. What was needed to end the feather trade, in addition to laws protecting birds?

7. How did those in the feather industry argue for its continuance?

8. How did the senator from Missouri view the proposal to protect migratory birds?

9. Why would it be inaccurate to describe the National Association of Audubon Societies as a **coterie**?

10. Why would a hat decorated with a complete owl be likely to appear **repugnant** to many people today?

FUN & FASCINATING FACTS

Flaunt means "to make a boastful display." *Flout* means "to treat with undisguised contempt." These two words have quite different meanings but have in common a disregard for what others might think. This may explain why they are sometimes misused in place of each other. A burglar may *flaunt* his ill-gotten gains, while *flouting* the laws that forbid his actions.

Don't confuse **demur,** which is a verb, with *demure*, which is an adjective and means "shy or modest in manner or behavior."

Lesson 16

Word List
Study the definitions of the words below; then do the exercises for the lesson.

archives
är´ kīvz

n. pl. Public or institutional records, especially historical documents that are preserved; the place where such records are kept.
We discovered the date our house was built by searching the town **archives**.

chattel
chat´ l

n. 1. An item of property that can be moved, as distinct from real estate.
The family **chattels** put up for sale included cattle, horses, furniture, and farm implements.
2. A human being considered as property.
In 73 B.C. Spartacus along with 90,000 other Roman **chattels** began a rebellion against their owners.

commodious
kə mō´ dē əs

adj. Having plenty of space to move around freely; roomy.
The **commodious** hotel room had space for two double beds without seeming crowded.

conflagration
kän flə grā´ shən

n. A large, disastrous fire.
In 1871 much of Chicago burned in a terrible **conflagration**.

limbo
lim´ bō

n. A place or state of neglect, oblivion, or transition.
Ivelisse's hopes of promotion were in **limbo** while management restructured the company.

lineage
lin´ ē ij

n. Line of descent; ancestry.
When Josh traced his **lineage**, he discovered that many of his ancestors had been farmers.

listless
list´ ləs

adj. Indifferent, spiritless; showing a lack of motivation or interest.
LeRon greeted me with a halfhearted hello and a **listless** handshake.
listlessness *n.*
Mr. Winters suspected that his daughter's **listlessness** indicated an incipient illness.

metropolis
mə träp´ ə lis

n. An important city, especially one regarded as the center of a particular activity.
Washington, D.C., may have started as a small town, but it is now a thriving **metropolis**.
metropolitan *adj.*
The **metropolitan** New York area includes parts of New Jersey, Long Island, and Westchester County.

perfunctory
pər fuŋk´ tər ē

adj. Done in a routine way, without care or particular interest.
My mother was so immersed in her work that she gave me only a **perfunctory** nod when I came into her office.

pristine
pris tēn´

adj. Like new; spotless; free of dirt and decay.
The city looked **pristine** under a thick blanket of freshly fallen snow.

ramshackle
ram´ shak əl

adj. Loosely made; appearing ready to collapse; dilapidated.
The **ramshackle** condition of the abandoned mansion was evident from the crumbling plaster in the once-elegant dining room.

sequester
sē kwes´ tər

v. 1. To set apart; to seclude.
Game-show contestants were **sequestered** in a soundproof booth.
2. To seize, especially by legal authority.
The police found the cache of illegal weapons and **sequestered** them, storing them in the evidence room at headquarters.

subversive
səb vʉr´ siv

adj. Planning to undermine or overthrow an established order.
The Alien and Sedition Acts of 1798 allowed the president to deport anyone he deemed a **subversive** influence on the U.S. government.
subvert *v.* To undermine the morals, authority, or allegiance of.
Critics of rock music often claim that it **subverts** the morals of its listeners.

terminus
tʉr´ mə nəs

n. The final destination or goal of a journey or endeavor; the finishing point.
I set out from Paris for Strasburg, the **terminus** of my journey.

virulent
vir´ yo͞o lənt

adj. 1. Extremely harmful or poisonous; deadly.
A **virulent** strain of flu attacked both the very young and the very old.
2. Full of hate; bitter or spiteful.
Despite the **virulent** criticism of her last book, the author exuded confidence as she walked to the podium.

16A Understanding Meanings

Read the sentences below. If a sentence correctly uses the word in bold, write *C* on the line below it. If a sentence is incorrect, rewrite it so that the vocabulary word in bold is used correctly.

1. One's **lineage** is the line of one's ancestors.

_____

2. A **virulent** infection is one that quickly breaks down the body's defenses.

archives
chattel
commodious
conflagration
limbo
lineage
listless
metropolis
perfunctory
pristine
ramshackle
sequester
subversive
terminus
virulent

_____

3. **Chattels** are slaves.

_____

4. A **terminus** is the duration of a politician's time in office.

_____

5. A **metropolis** is a view over a wide area.

_____

6. To be in **limbo** is to be in a state of enforced activity.

7. A **commodious** hall is one with room for many people.

8. To **sequester** someone is to share a secret with that person.

9. A **ramshackle** structure is one that is buttressed for strength.

10. **Archives** were an ancient seafaring people.

11. To **subvert** an existing order is to overthrow it completely.

12. A **conflagration** is a large outdoor gathering.

13. A **perfunctory** examination is one that is not very thorough.

14. A **listless** person is one who is poorly organized.

15. A **pristine** stream is one that is pure and clean.

16B Using Words

If the word (or a form of the word) in bold fits in a sentence in the group below it, write the word in the blank. If the word does not fit, leave the space empty.

1. **terminus**

   (a) Dad was mortified when a _____ crawled across the kitchen ceiling.

   (b) Mt. Katahdin, in Maine, is the northern _____ of the 2,000-mile Appalachian Trail.

   (c) The train was twenty minutes late arriving at its _____ .

2. **virulent**

   (a) The actors were stung by a _____ review from the local drama critic.

   (b) Scientists have identified a new and more _____ strain of the virus.

   (c) After working out three times a week for a year, she was in _____ health.

3. **lineage**

   (a) Until she conducted a search, Meredith's _____ remained a mystery to her.

   (b) The British royal family can trace its _____ back a thousand years.

   (c) Owners of thoroughbred racehorses keep complete records of their animals' _____ .

4. **archives**

   (a) The original draft of the U.S. Constitution is kept in the National _____ .

   (b) The town _____ contain land deeds going back to the 1680s.

   (c) Vonda studied her class _____ from the previous semester to prepare for the test.

5. **subversive**

   (a) The government claimed the right to ban what it deemed _____ organizations.

   (b) The rank of captain is _____ to that of major in the army or air force.

   (c) Critics claim that excessive movie violence is _____ of the nation's values.

6. **sequester**

   (a) Saroie _____ herself in her room for hours to practice the guitar.

   (b) The state _____ the vessel that had been used to smuggle illegal drugs.

   (c) The twins were _____ at birth and didn't meet until twenty years later.

7. **commodious**

   (a) The trunk was _____ enough to contain all Donna's possessions.

   (b) The landlord was _____ to our request for a slight reduction in the rent.

   (c) Rio de Janeiro's _____ harbor makes it attractive to even the largest cruise ships.

archives
chattel
commodious
conflagration
limbo
lineage
listless
metropolis
perfunctory
pristine
ramshackle
sequester
subversive
terminus
virulent

8. **pristine**

    (a) The hotel manager took pride in the restaurant's _____ table linens.

    (b) A small army of groundskeepers keep the park in _____ condition.

    (c) Clark was careful to do nothing that might sully his _____ driving record.

16C Word Study

Choose from the two words provided and use each word only once when filling in the spaces. One space should be left blank.

genesis/beginning

1. The _____ of the Mississippi is located in Lake Itasca, which is in Minnesota.

2. I read the book from _____ to end in less than an hour.

3. The _____ of her interest in moths can be traced back to a childhood incident.

sundered/severed

4. Juan _____ the rope with one swift stroke of the knife.

5. Britain was _____ into two factions, one led by Cromwell, the other by Charles I.

6. With a coffee grinder we _____ the beans into a fine powder.

sequestered/secluded

7. Amy is a very _____ person, and it takes a while to get to know her.

8. Members of the panel were _____ while they investigated the incident.

9. We found a _____ spot by a lake where we had a picnic.

transcend/surpass

10. This year's sales will _____ last year's by a whopping twenty percent.

11. If you _____ the Busby School, you'll know you've gone too far.

12. By constant meditation, he seeks to _____ the world of everyday things.

virulent/deadly

13. I was feeling particularly _____ that morning.

14. Many diseases that were once _____ can now be avoided by having the proper inoculations.

15. The speaker's remarks were so _____ that we were all taken aback.

16D Images of Words

Circle the letter of each sentence that suggests the numbered bold vocabulary word. In each group, you may circle more than one letter or none at all.

1. **listless**

   (a) The class began to fidget midway through Mr. Murdock's dreary lecture.

   (b) The patient barely responded when the doctor shone a light in his eyes.

   (c) Ms. Ingram's son slumped in an armchair and took no interest in her suggestions.

2. **pristine**

   (a) Robin's manner was so prim that her classmates teased her.

   (b) The 1923 automobile had been perfectly restored to its original condition.

   (c) James hesitated before applying the first stroke of paint to the expanse of white canvas.

3. **conflagration**

   (a) The huge tsunami pulverized buildings along the coast.

   (b) We sat around the roaring fire, roasting chestnuts and telling stories.

   (c) The Great Fire of London in 1666 virtually destroyed the city.

4. **ramshackle**

   (a) Barry's tree house was haphazardly constructed from scrap pieces.

   (b) The sheep was confined to his pen by means of a chain and metal collar.

   (c) Many houses in historic Williamsburg, Virginia, were in a sad state before their restoration.

5. **chattel**

   (a) The owner was offering the land for ten thousand dollars an acre.

   (b) The entire contents of the house sold for eight thousand dollars.

   (c) Men, women, and children were confined in the cramped, filthy holds of the slave ship.

6. **archives**

   (a) Excavated dinosaur bones tell us much about the distant past.

   (b) A framed letter, signed "A. Einstein," hung on the study wall.

   (c) My research revealed that the town founders had emigrated from Norway.

7. **subvert**

   (a) Termites had weakened the wood foundation, making the house unstable.

   (b) Xa Chou's recent absence spoiled his perfect attendance record.

   (c) A series of mild heart attacks made Mrs. Schultz-McGuire decide to take early retirement.

archives
chattel
commodious
conflagration
limbo
lineage
listless
metropolis
perfunctory
pristine
ramshackle
sequester
subversive
terminus
virulent

8. **sequester**

   (a) I took a clean sheet of paper and divided it into two-inch squares.

   (b) During the trial, jurors were isolated in a hotel and monitored closely by the court officers.

   (c) Separate the egg whites from the yolks and beat them until stiff.

9. **metropolis**

   (a) Hillsdale consisted of two dozen houses, a gas station, and a diner.

   (b) It was Joe's first visit to New York, and its size overwhelmed him.

   (c) Kazumi's knowledge of many languages led her to consider herself a citizen of the world rather than of any particular place.

10. **limbo**

   (a) The restaurant's opening is on hold until the menu can be finalized.

   (b) Simone and Grace waited in line for over five hours to buy tickets to the Metal Dogz concert.

   (c) Refugees in the camp had no idea when they would be free to return home.

16E Passage

Read the passage below; then complete the exercise that follows it.

Gateway to the Promised Land

Trace your **lineage** back three or four generations and you may well find that you are one of the hundred million Americans descended from immigrants who came to the United States by way of Ellis Island. This small plot of land in New York harbor was the **terminus** on a long ocean journey of millions of people from around the world who came here seeking freedom and prosperity. Once past inspection on Ellis Island, they were free to move on to their final destinations, one-third of them going no farther than New York, the great **metropolis** that lay a mile to the north, the other two-thirds fanning out to every part of the country.

The federal government assumed responsibility for immigration from the individual states in 1891, and the following year began using Ellis Island to process would-be residents. This was a logical choice, since New York City was the destination for many of those arriving from Europe, and the deep harbor allowed steamships to dock easily.

Between 1892 and 1924, twelve million people passed through Ellis Island at a rate that often exceeded five thousand a day. With such a vast number of people, it was miraculous that the **conflagration** of 1897, which destroyed the original wooden buildings, took no lives.

In the Baggage Room just inside the main entrance, new arrivals deposited the few **chattels** they had brought, in tied-up bundles and battered suitcases. From there they proceeded to the Registry Room, a **commodious** hall on the second floor where immigration officials decided who would and who would not be admitted to the new country.

Candidates for residence had to be mentally competent, able to support themselves, and in reasonably good health. Only one in fifty was denied entry, usually for medical reasons or because the inspectors considered them politically **subversive** and therefore unwelcome. From the head of the stairs in the Registry Room doctors studied the people as they ascended, looking for signs of **listlessness** or shortness of breath that might indicate heart or lung disease. Those about whom there were legal or medical doubts were **sequestered** on the third floor. They remained there in **limbo** for weeks or even months until their cases were decided. Most, however, passed through in three to five hours and were sent on their way, the **perfunctory** medical examinations seldom taking more than sixty seconds to complete. However, people suffering from illnesses such as trachoma, a particularly **virulent** eye disease that spreads rapidly and can cause blindness, were automatically denied entry.

By 1954, the rate of immigration had slowed considerably, and steamships were giving way to airliners. The immigration offices on Ellis Island had to be closed. In 1965, the island was incorporated as part of the nearby Statute of Liberty National Monument, but was not maintained. Ten years later, triggered by concern over the buildings' **ramshackle** condition, the Ellis Island Restoration Project was begun. Private donations totaling $160 million allowed the main brick and limestone building to be restored to its former **pristine** condition, and for construction within it of a museum honoring America's immigrant tradition.

It opened to the public in 1990 as the Ellis Island Museum of Immigration, boasting exhibits, artifacts, films, **archives**, and a research library. One of its most popular features is the Ellis Island Oral History Project, which has been conducting interviews since 1973, and has amassed more than 1,300 firsthand accounts of the immigrant experience. These are accessible to visitors via twenty computer terminals, where users can see the faces and hear the stories of men and women who passed through Ellis Island on their way to what, for many, was indeed the promised land.

Answer each of the following questions in the form of a sentence. If a question does not contain a vocabulary word from this lesson's word list, use one in your answer. Use each word only once.

1. What was the **terminus** for about one-third of the immigrants arriving at Ellis Island at the beginning of the twentieth century?

2. Do the original buildings on Ellis Island still exist? Why or why not?

3. What advantages did Ellis Island have as a reception point for immigrants?

archives
chattel
commodious
conflagration
limbo
lineage
listless
metropolis
perfunctory
pristine
ramshackle
sequester
subversive
terminus
virulent

4. Do you think the **chattel** people bring today differs from that of a century ago? Explain your answer.

5. Why is it unlikely that today one's energy level is an important factor in determining immigrant status?

6. What do you think might have been the worst part of being kept in **limbo**?

7. What kinds of people were not admitted to the country?

8. Why did the buildings at Ellis Island become **ramshackle**?

9. How might people find out if their ancestors came through Ellis Island?

10. Why is it unlikely that Native Americans would search the records at Ellis Island for their ancestors?

FUN & FASCINATING FACTS

Archives is usually a plural noun, whether it refers to a collection of documents or to the building where such a collection is housed. This word and *oligarchy* (Lesson 15) share the same Greek root *arkhe*, "government." The Greek *archeion*, from which *archives* is derived, means "government house." An *oligarchy* is a government run by a few people, usually members of a country's most powerful families.

In Roman Catholic theology, *Limbo* was a place where souls remained. These souls could not enter heaven but did not deserve consignment to hell. The term comes from the Latin *limbus*, "a border." Limbo was thought to border on heaven or hell but was not a part of either. The term extended its meaning so that **limbo** is now any transitional, neglected, or confined state.

Review for Lessons 13–16

Hidden Message In the boxes provided, write the words from Lessons 13 through 16 that are missing in each of the sentences below. The number following each sentence gives the word list from which the missing word is taken. When the exercise is finished, the shaded boxes will spell out a quotation from famed scientist Albert Einstein.

1. Aunt Doris was appalled by Uncle Bill's _____ table manners. (13)

2. Everyone laughed at Bernie's _____ idea. (15)

3. Several _____ issues must also be considered. (15)

4. This one-sided proposal is _____ to our interests. (15)

5. The dancer's _____ movements enthralled us. (14)

6. Huang gave the note a _____ glance. (16)

7. Lagos, Nigeria, was the _____ of Ms. Sikorsky's journey. (16)

8. A small _____ of friends advised the president. (15)

9. Andrew _____ed his friendships with important people. (15)

10. The illness has left Miya feeling _____ . (16)

11. It's unfair to quote someone out of _____ . (13)

12. Allow me to be the _____ of the dispute. (15)

13. Before developers took over, the island was _____ . (16)

14. The speech consisted of one _____ after another. (13)

15. The _____ of the royal family is known in detail. (16)

16. Martin's confidence is a(n) _____ to hide his insecurity. (14)

17. It's impossible to _____ these two sets of facts. (13)

18. Your friendship helped Tina shake off her _____ . (13)

19. I was _____ when it came to answering my mail. (14)

20. Do no harm is a(n) _____ of the medical profession. (14)

21. A(n) _____ of heads of state meets tomorrow. (15)

22. A miser never experiences the joy of _____ . (13)

23. French _____ makes heavy use of rich sauces. (13)

24. A(n) _____ trunk held all my possessions. (16)

25. Can a lightning bolt _____ a rock of this size? (13)

26. Freedom of the press is _____ in a democracy. (14)

27. By 1800, New York was a major _____ . (16)

28. More sandbags were needed to _____ the levee. (14)

29. Please state your objections if you _____ . (15)

30. My birthday and Passover are _____ this year. (13)

31. Do nothing to _____ the high office you hold. (13)

32. Until a decision is made, we are left in _____ . (16)

33. The _____ towered over the other buildings. (14)

34. Leah _____ me to the party with promises of cake. (15)

35. Our common humanity should _____ all borders. (14)

36. His _____ description made a vivid impression. (15)

37. The _____ begins with a slow, solemn movement. (14)

38. In its most _____ form the disease is fatal. (16)

39. We _____ you to appear before the board. (13)

40. Those in _____ prayed for relief from their misery. (13)

41. Such acts were deemed _____ and were banned. (16)

42. George took a(n) _____ amount of time to prepare. (15)

43. Such a(n) _____ team will be hard to beat. (15)

44. Work is in _____ until the permits are obtained. (14)

45. A goblet of bubbling liquid was offered as a(n) _____ . (13)

46. The _____ 's features were grotesque. (14)

47. Miami will be the _____ for this year's Super Bowl. (14)

48. The law can _____ property believed to be stolen. (16)

49. We searched the _____ looking for the deed. (16)

50. General Shu was invited to join the ruling _____ . (15)

51. In law, any item of furniture is deemed a(n) _____ . (16)

52. If both parties drop charges, the case becomes _____ . (14)

53. The nanny's _____ manner impressed everyone. (15)

54. The _____ council includes Jews, Muslims, and Christians. (14)

55. The book explores the _____ of Gertrude Stein's ideas. (13)

Lesson 17

Word List

Study the definitions of the words below; then do the exercises for the lesson.

autocractic
ôt ə krat´ ik

adj. Exercising sole or complete control; dictatorial.
Critics accused the prosecutor of running the department in such an **autocratic** way that everyone was afraid to say anything.
autocrat *n.* One who exercises total control; a domineering person.
The queen ruled as an **autocrat** after abolishing Parliament.
autocracy *n.* (ô täk´ rə sē) Absolute rule by a single person.
Critics argue that while socialist in some ways, Cuba became more of an **autocracy** under Fidel Castro's firm hand.

caustic
kôs´ tik

adj. 1. Capable of destroying tissue by chemical action; corrosive.
Lye, used in soap making, is **caustic** enough to burn one's skin.
2. Very sarcastic; sharp or biting.
Ahmed tried to make his **caustic** remarks milder, but even his friends think he's incorrigible.

debilitate
dē bil´ ə tāt

v. To impair the strength of; to enfeeble.
Liza's long illness had so **debilitated** her that she was confined to bed.

duplicitous
do͞o plis´ ə təs

adj. Marked by deception.
A double agent cannot lead a simple and open life, but must always be **duplicitous**.
duplicity *n.* Deceit in speech or actions; deliberate deception.
The scam artist's **duplicity** was discovered before he made off with the money.

emissary
em´ ə ser ē

n. A representative sent on a special errand.
Emissaries from eight Asian countries convened in Tokyo to plan the economic summit.

felicitous
fə lis´ i təs

adj. 1. Happily suited to an occasion or situation; appropriate and graceful.
Though I was afraid Marcela would bungle the delicate matter, she dealt with it in a **felicitous** way.
2. Marked by happiness or good fortune; pleasant; charming.
Happily ensconced in their home in the country, the Robesons led a **felicitous** life.

forthright
fôrth´ rīt

adj. Direct; straightforward; frank.
Their classmates preferred Jermain's **forthright** manner to Rebecca's deceitful style.

impecunious
im pi kyo͞o´ nē əs

adj. Being habitually without money; poor.
Impecunious artists were sometimes willing to sell paintings for the price of a good meal.

jaundiced
jôn´ dist

adj. 1. Of an unhealthy yellow appearance.
Adam's **jaundiced** skin may indicate hepatitis.
2. Affected by jealousy, resentment, or hostility.
Relegated to a small cubicle, Renee cast a **jaundiced** eye on her friend's commodious corner office.

mercenary
mʉr´ sə ner ē

adj. Serving merely for money or gain; greedy.
In their **mercenary** concern for profits above community service, the shop owners raised their prices so that few local residents could afford them.
n. A soldier who fights for whoever pays him.
The aggrieved foreign **mercenaries** in the sultan's army threatened to switch sides unless they were paid promptly.

notorious
nō tôr´ ē əs

adj. Well known for a particular quality or trait, often an unfavorable one.
Bilal is **notorious** for his dilatory payment of bills.
notoriety   *n.* (nō tə rī´ ə tē)
Some gangsters seem to enjoy the **notoriety** associated with their lifestyle.

oust
oust

v. To eject from a position or place; to drive out of use.
No one demurred when a board member suggested that they **oust** the company president and replace her with a new one.
ouster *n.* Dismissal from a position.
Once discovered, the hapless president's improprieties resulted in his **ouster** from the company.

parsimonious
pär´ sə mō´ nē əs

adj. Excessively sparing or frugal; penurious.
Caleb's character was so **parsimonious** that he even denied his children an allowance.
parsimony   *n.* (pär´ sə mō nē)
Though Shantal had once made a habit of squandering money, she now lived a life of extreme **parsimony**.

pejorative
pi jôr´ ə tiv

adj. Having negative or unpleasant associations; belittling.
"Philistine" is admittedly a **pejorative** term, but I think it fits Yasmin perfectly.

precept
prē´ sept

n. A general principle or rule of action.
Guided by the **precept** "Less is more," she designed her house in a spare but striking style.

17A Understanding Meanings

Read the sentences below. If a sentence correctly uses the word in bold, write *C* on the line below it. If a sentence is incorrect, rewrite it so that the vocabulary word in bold is used correctly.

1. A **felicitous** greeting is one that is gracefully expressed.

_____

autocratic
caustic
debilitate
duplicitous
emissary
felicitous
forthright
impecunious
jaundiced
mercenary
notorious
oust
parsimonious
pejorative
precept

2. A **pejorative** term is one that is flattering.

_____

3. A **notorious** person is one with a bad reputation.

_____

4. To **oust** someone is to expel that person from a position or place.

_____

5. A **mercenary** is a sum of money paid for a service or product.

_____

6. A **jaundiced** look is one expressing envy or resentment.

7. A **caustic** substance is one that has therapeutic qualities.

8. An **autocrat** is a spoiled child.

9. **Parsimony** is extreme penny-pinching.

10. To be **debilitated** is to be in a weakened state.

11. A **forthright** person is one who speaks plainly.

12. **Duplicity** is a state of confusion.

13. An **impecunious** person is one who has no money.

14. An **emissary** is something given off, as a smell or sound.

15. A **precept** is a rule governing conduct.

17B Using Words

If the word (or a form of the word) in bold fits in a sentence in the group below it, write the word in the blank. If the word does not fit, leave the space empty.

1. debilitate

(a) Lamar was so _____ to credit card companies that he considered declaring bankruptcy.

(b) The country's economy was _____ by corruption and mismanagement.

(c) Constant criticism had so _____ Bill's self-esteem that he felt worthless.

2. impecunious

(a) Grandma has been in _____ health for some time but is slowly recovering.

(b) Wealthy Uncle Theo was beset by _____ relatives asking him for loans.

(c) Walter offered her an _____ bunch of wildflowers picked from a vacant lot.

3. parsimonious

(a) Ernest Hemingway was _____ in his use of adjectives.

(b) So _____ was Silas that parting with a dollar caused him actual pain.

(c) I caught Aunt Anita in a _____ mood and came away empty-handed.

4. notorious

(a) This part of town was once _____ for its high crime rate.

(b) Josh was successful in concealing his _____ ideas from his friends.

(c) Bureaucrats are _____ for jealously guarding their turf.

5. jaundiced

(a) With proper treatment, Carla's _____ pallor soon gave way to a healthy glow.

(b) The whites of the eyes becoming _____ is a symptom of hepatitis.

(c) Ming's _____ comments suggests he does not view our proposal favorably.

6. oust

(a) The senators' plan to _____ the secretary of state soon became known.

(b) The merging of the two banks threatens to _____ hundreds from their jobs.

(c) The _____ of the Yankees' manager failed to stop the team's losing streak.

7. caustic

(a) Sulfuric acid is a _____ substance that burns on contact with the skin.

(b) The movie is a _____ satire on the influence of money in politics.

(c) The earthquake was _____ by the movement of sections of the planet's crust.

autocratic
caustic
debilitate
duplicitious
emissary
felicitous
forthright
impecunious
jaundiced
mercenary
notorious
oust
parsimonious
pejorative
precept

8. **felicitous**

    (a) The request was made in so _____ a manner that I couldn't refuse.

    (b) Mrs. Cardosa was thankful to have lived a long, useful, and _____ life.

    (c) The synthetic fur felt almost as _____ as the real thing.

17C Word Study

Fill in the missing word in each of the sentences below. Then write a brief definition of the word. The number in parentheses gives the lesson from which the word is taken.

1. The prefix *com-* means "with." It combines with the Latin *mensus* (measured)

    to form the English word _____ (14), meaning

    _____ .

2. The prefix *im-* means "not." It combines with the Latin *pecunia* (wealth)

    to form the English word _____ (17), meaning

    _____ .

3. The prefix *trans-* means "across." It combines with the Latin *scandere* (to climb)

    to form the English word _____ (14), meaning

    _____ .

4. The Latin *mater* (mother) and *polis* (city) combine to form

    the English word _____ (16), meaning

    _____ .

5. The prefix *dis-* means "apart." It combines with the Latin *latus* (carried)

    to form the English word _____ (14), meaning

    _____ .

6. The Greek *oligos* (few) and *archi* (rule) combine to form

    the English word _____ (15), meaning

    _____ .

7. The prefix *con-* means "with." It combines with the Latin *comitari* (to accompany)

    to form the English word _____ (15), meaning

    _____ .

8. The prefix *de-* means "away." It combines with the Latin *morari* (to delay) to form the English word _____ (15), meaning

_____ .

9. The prefix *con-* means "with." It combines with the Latin *clavis* (key) to form the English word _____ (15), meaning

_____ .

10. The Latin *pinna* (feather) forms the English word _____ (14), meaning

_____ .

17D Images of Words

Circle the letter of each sentence that suggests the numbered bold vocabulary word. In each group, you may circle more than one letter or none at all.

1. **felicitous**

   (a) Mark is always ready with a pleasant remark at the right moment.

   (b) The July 4th display of red, white, and blue flowers was appropriate.

   (c) April expressed her regret at not being able to attend the party.

2. **mercenary**

   (a) The term "Hessians" refers to all German soldiers hired by the British during the American Revolution.

   (b) Dr. Samuel Johnson said that the only reason to write was to make money.

   (c) With no serious competition, the store raised prices outrageously.

3. **parsimony**

   (a) The church condemned the lending of money at excessive rates of interest.

   (b) Auntie Natalie gave me a quarter for my birthday and advised me not to spend it.

   (c) Cal wasn't hungry and pushed away his steaming plate of food.

4. **forthright**

   (a) The road stretched straight ahead with neither bend nor fork in sight.

   (b) They put up a valiant struggle but were forced to yield in the end.

   (c) With Emily, you always know exactly where you stand.

5. **precept**

   (a) Tom Paine maintained that "my country is the world and my religion is to do good."

   (b) Father suggested that I not spend all my money on vacation.

   (c) Bailey avoided eating meat whenever possible.

autocratic
caustic
debilitate
duplicitous
emissary
felicitous
forthright
impecunious
jaundiced
mercenary
notorious
oust
parsimonious
pejorative
precept

6. duplicity

(a) Isis could look you in the eye and convince you she was telling the truth.

(b) Giles had a very bad habit of saying one thing and doing another.

(c) The dealer told me the car was "guaranteed," but didn't say for how long.

7. emissary

(a) Car and truck exhaust contains poisonous carbon monoxide.

(b) Marco Polo traveled to distant parts of China on Kublai Khan's business.

(c) The message revealed that Mother was ill and urged me to come at once.

8. autocratic

(a) Once it is switched on, the machinery runs by itself.

(b) The political careers of those who disagreed with the majority leader were put in jeopardy.

(c) Ms. Evans ran the firm as she pleased, without consulting her employees.

9. pejorative

(a) Lydia found the term "poetess" offensive, preferring "poet" instead.

(b) George Herman Ruth was commonly known as "Babe Ruth."

(c) When Gerald asked what a sawbuck is, I told him that it is a ten-dollar bill.

10. impecunious

(a) The house was badly in need of a coat of paint, and the garden was a mess.

(b) Mr. Mauriac claimed that his bad back prevented him from working.

(c) Ms. Barton's poor judgment led her to hire people who lacked qualifications.

17E Passage

Read the passage below; then complete the exercise that follows it.

Machiavelli

When someone behaves in a way that is politically shrewd or **duplicitous**, or acts in bad faith, we may describe that person as *Machiavellian*. The word comes from the name of Niccolò Machiavelli, an Italian diplomat and administrator who lived from 1460 to 1527. In addition to his governmental duties in the city-state of Florence, he was a prolific author, and his **felicitous** prose style places him in the forefront of Italian writers. Machiavelli's works include histories, comic plays, and treatises on war, politics, and diplomacy, but he has become famous, or perhaps **notorious**, because of a single book—his brutally honest handbook for rulers called *The Prince*.

Machiavelli was born in Florence at a time when the many Italian city-states were in a condition of almost continuous war. Florence had long been a republic where citizens participated in government, but in 1469, the year of Machiavelli's birth, it came under the control of Lorenzo de' Medici, known as Lorenzo the Magnificent. He was an extremely cruel yet highly cultivated man under whose **autocratic** rule the arts flourished. France invaded northern Italy in 1494, helping the Florentines **oust** the Medici family; for the next two decades the city was once again a republic (in fact as well as in name).

After the Medici departed, Machiavelli served in Florence's government. Though he had been born into a distinguished family, he found himself in **impecunious** circumstances because his father had incurred large debts that he was unable to repay. Machiavelli found employment as a clerk of the republic and quickly proved his worth. He was elected several times to the chancery, the ruling body of Florence, and served as its **emissary** on important missions to France, Germany, and Rome. He played a major role in forming a citizen army to replace the fickle **mercenary** bands that Florence had previously relied on for its defense.

In 1512, a Spanish army loyal to the pope, with whom the Medici had close ties, conquered the city and ended French influence. Machiavelli's beloved Florence had fallen despite his efforts to improve its defenses. The Medici were restored to power, and Machiavelli's political career ended abruptly. After being tortured and incarcerated as a suspected traitor, he was eventually allowed to retire to his small property just outside the city, where he devoted himself to writing.

Deeply affected by the fall of Florence and disturbed by the disunited state in which Italy found itself, Machiavelli sought in *The Prince* (1513) to answer this question: What were the qualities of a strong leader, one who could successfully defend his own territory, secure his power, and achieve his goals? The book contains many **precepts** that deal straightforwardly with the holding and wielding of political power. It advises the ruler who wishes to retain his position to be ruthless in exercising power. Ideally, a ruler should be both loved and feared, but, as Machiavelli states in his usual **forthright** manner, this is seldom possible. In that case, he concludes, then it is better that the ruler be feared.

Perhaps reacting to Lorenzo's extravagances, he also advises the wise ruler to be **parsimonious** in public spending and allow his people to prosper on their own, with one exception: A ruler can be generous in granting the spoils of victory to his successful army, but only when the proceeds come from the defeated enemy. While earlier political philosophers had judged rulers by the morality of their actions, Machiavelli argued that morality and religion were simply tools to be used as the ruler saw fit. Though a religious man, he believed that Christianity applied to warfare had a **debilitating** effect on the military virtues. Some scholars believe that this **jaundiced** view of human nature came from his observations of the diplomatic and political intrigues of his day.

These views shocked the Catholic hierarchy and many of the faithful. Machiavelli's outspoken, often **caustic**, opinions sometimes made him unpopular, especially with those who did not realize that he wanted to shock his readers by appearing more wicked than he was. The French coined the word *Machiavellianism* as a **pejorative** term, possibly influenced by their animosity toward Italy and things Italian. Ultimately, whether *The Prince* reflects Machiavelli's own morality or is simply a candid discussion of the qualities a ruler needs in turbulent times is a question historians and readers must answer for themselves.

Answer each of the following questions in the form of a sentence. If a question does not contain a vocabulary word from this lesson's word list, use one in your answer. Use each word only once.

autocratic

caustic

debilitate

duplicitous

emissary

felicitous

forthright

impecunious

jaundiced

mercenary

notorious

oust

parsimonious

pejorative

precept

1. Why was the period of Lorenzo de' Medici's rule a **felicitous** time for artists?

_____

2. How did the government that succeeded Lorenzo's rule differ from his?

_____

3. What is one way to describe Machiavelli's writings?

_____

4. What details in the passage suggest that Lorenzo de' Medici may have brought Florence to an **impecunious** state?

_____

5. When he worked in government, what was one of Machiavelli's contributions to Florence?

6. From the description of Machiavelli's ideas provided in the passage, do you think his **notoriety** is deserved? Explain your answer.

7. What happened to Machiavelli when French rule ended in 1512?

8. Why did the Catholic church view Machiavelli unfavorably?

9. What events mentioned in the passage might account for Machiavelli's **jaundiced** view of human society?

10. Do you think a **parsimonious** ruler could have a **debilitating** effect on his country? Explain your answer.

FUN & FASCINATING FACTS

The prefix *auto-*, from the Greek *autos*, "self," and the Greek root *kratos*, "power," combine to form the word **autocracy**. Several other words share the root *kratos*. It combines with *aristos*, "best," to form *aristocracy*, "government by the best," and with *demos*, "people," to form *democracy*, "government by the people." A recent coinage is *meritocracy*, "government by those who show merit."

In the early days of Rome, wealth was measured by the number of farm animals, or *pecus*, a person owned.

The meaning broadened to include all kinds of wealth, including money, and then came to be applied to money in particular. The adjective form, *pecuniary*, means "pertaining to money." (A lawyer with a *pecuniary* interest in a case hopes to make money from it.) By adding the prefix *im-*, "not," we get **impecunious**, "lacking money."

The words **notorious** and **notoriety** once both referred to being well known in either a positive *or* a negative way. In recent usage, both words have come to refer to a negative, unsavory reputation.

Lesson 18

Word List
Study the definitions of the words below; then do the exercises for the lesson.

bereft
bē reft´
adj. Deprived of or lacking something that is wanted or needed.
The flood waters left residents of Great Rapids **bereft** of home and possessions.

criterion
krī tir´ ē ən
n. A standard or rule by which something is judged or criticized.
criteria *n.* pl.
The **criteria** on which a diamond is rated are clarity, carat, color, and cut.

deride
di rīd´
v. To laugh at in scorn or contempt; to ridicule.
Laughing sarcastically, the coach **derided** the players for their lackluster performance in the game's first quarter.
derision *n.*
Ira's hackneyed speech earned the **derision** of his scornful classmates.

effrontery
e frun´ tər ē
n. A boldness that is offensive because of its lack of tact; audacity.
Mrs. Bell had the **effrontery** to announce that she was appalled by the amount of trash we generated each week.

espouse
e spouz´
v. To advocate or embrace, especially a cause or idea.
In his 1903 book *The Souls of Black Folk*, W. E. B. DuBois **espoused** self-determination and independence for African Americans.
espousal *n.*
Ang's **espousal** of alien abduction theories estranged her from her friends.

hypocrisy
hi päk´ rə sē
n. The practice of pretending to believe or value things or ideas that one does not; falseness.
The book attacked the **hypocrisy** of companies who promoted their products abroad after they had been banned as harmful to human health in the United States.
hypocrite *n.* (hip´ ə krit) A person who pretends to be what he or she is not or to have principles he or she does not possess.
A **hypocrite** will pretend generosity while practicing parsimony.
hypocritical *adj.*
Daria supposed it would be rather **hypocritical** of her to skip class after having chastised her brother for that very thing.

impending
im pen´ diŋ
adj. About to occur; imminent.
The **impending** storm put our weekend travel plans in limbo.

incensed
in senst´
adj. Filled with wrath; enraged.
Kurt was so **incensed** upon discovering Omar's mistake that he berated him for a full five minutes.

pertinent
pur´ tə nənt
adj. Relating to the matter at hand; relevant.
The facts you present, while interesting, are not **pertinent** to our topic of study.

promulgate
präm´ əl gāt
v. To proclaim or make known.
The department has **promulgated** to all employees new guidelines to prevent sexual harassment in the workplace.

proscribe prō skrīb´	*v.* To forbid as harmful; to prohibit. Obstetricians **proscribe** the drinking of alcoholic beverages by pregnant women.
redress rē dres´	*v.* To correct or compensate for a wrong. The mayor lost the election for failing to **redress** grievances concerning city schools. *n.* Something that makes up for a wrong. Japanese Americans who had been confined to camps during WW II were given monetary compensation as **redress** for this wrong.
regime rā zhēm´	*n.* A form of rule or government. The military **regime** replied with an unequivocal "no" when its opponents proposed free elections.
retribution re trə byōō´ shən	*n.* Something given in repayment, especially punishment; recompense. The lawyer sought **retribution** for those involved in the accident.
substantiate səb stan´ shē āt	*v.* To verify or confirm by presenting evidence. A deed **substantiates** ownership of a property.

18A Understanding Meanings

Read the sentences below. If a sentence correctly uses the word in bold, write *C* on the line below it. If a sentence is incorrect, rewrite it so that the vocabulary word in bold is used correctly.

1. **Effrontery** is a feeling of vague uneasiness.

_____

2. A **regime** is a system of government.

_____

3. To **espouse** something is to take it up as a cause.

_____

4. A **hypocritical** person pretends to hold beliefs he or she does not possess.

_____

5. To **substantiate** a claim is to show proof in support of it.

_____

6. To **redress** a wrong is to make it worse.

_____

7. To be **bereft** of something is to suffer the loss of it.

_____

8. To **deride** someone is to flatter that person.

_____

9. A **pertinent** comment is saucy and rather bold.

_____

10. **Retribution** is punishment for a wrongdoing.

_____

11. To **proscribe** something is to recommend or require its use.

_____

12. A **criterion** is an evaluation or judgment of a work of art.

_____

13. An **impending** decision is one that is binding on those affected by it.

_____

14. To **promulgate** a ruling is to officially announce it.

_____

15. An **incensed** person is one who is very angry.

_____

bereft
criterion
deride
effrontery
espouse
hypocrisy
impending
incensed
pertinent
promulgate
proscribe
redress
regime
retribution
substantiate

18B Using Words

If the word (or a form of the word) in bold fits in a sentence in the group below it, write the word in the blank space. If the word does not fit, leave the space empty.

1. **incensed**

(a) I was _____ when my roommate used my car without so much as asking.

(b) The show was so bad that the _____ patrons demanded their money back.

(c) You can't blame the baby for being _____ when she's very hungry.

2. **promulgate**

   (a) The publishers hope to _____ the book by early November.

   (b) Evangelists _____ their religious views through television and radio.

   (c) The government expects to _____ the new tax code by the end of the year.

3. **espouse**

   (a) Doctors _____ a weight-loss program of reduced fat intake and moderate exercise.

   (b) What do you _____ is the reason for Andrea's peculiar behavior?

   (c) Most Americans _____ the principle of separation of church and state.

4. **pertinent**

   (a) The points you raise are _____ , and I will address them in a moment.

   (b) Roslyn's _____ manner can mislead people into thinking she is impolite.

   (c) I have some information that I believe is _____ to your inquiries.

5. **bereft**

   (a) The economy was in such a shambles that paper money was _____ of value.

   (b) They must have been _____ of their senses to fall for a trick like that.

   (c) Too many high school graduates see a future _____ of opportunities.

6. **hypocritical**

   (a) It is _____ for U.S. senators to rail against the federal government.

   (b) To criticize rent control while living in rent-controlled housing is _____ .

   (c) My sister is extremely _____ of the friends I choose.

7. **proscribe**

   (a) Both the Muslim Koran and the Jewish Talmud _____ the eating of pork.

   (b) Several countries _____ advertising tobacco products on television.

   (c) The doctor can _____ an antibiotic for your illness.

8. **deride**

   (a) Shakespeare _____ his English history plays from Holinshed's Chronicles.

   (b) Critics _____ the early impressionist painters as slapdash and uncouth.

   (c) Philistines _____ art that they do not understand.

18C Word Study

Each group of four words below contains two words that are either synonyms or antonyms. Circle these two words, then circle the *S* if they are synonyms, the *A* if they are antonyms.

1. beneficial	inimical	implacable	concomitant	S	A
2. ramshackle	vibrant	listless	bereft	S	A

3. subversive	filthy	pristine	hapless	S	A
4. cramped	commodious	virulent	eclectic	S	A
5. weaken	oust	incensed	debilitate	S	A
6. fearful	notorious	corrosive	caustic	S	A
7. munificent	perfunctory	pertinent	parsimonious	S	A
8. bellicose	aware	forthright	duplicitous	S	A
9. emissary	ouster	appointment	tenet	S	A
10. adulation	retribution	redress	derision	S	A

18D Images of Words

Circle the letter of each sentence that suggests the numbered bold vocabulary word. In each group, you may circle more than one letter or none at all.

1. **criterion**

   (a) The highest position in the House of Representatives is that of Speaker.

   (b) Students' SAT scores are one way to judge a school's performance.

   (c) We compare sprinters by measuring how fast they can run 100 meters.

2. **impending**

   (a) This tray contains documents on which no action has yet been taken.

   (b) The day before the attack on Pearl Harbor was no different than any other.

   (c) The prisoner had marked off the days remaining before his release.

3. **retribution**

   (a) Every voter in the district received a copy of the candidate's position paper.

   (b) In the Bible, Lot's wife disobeyed God's order and was turned into a pillar of salt.

   (c) Mr. Scott offered to replace the neighbor's window his son had inadvertently broken.

4. **espouse**

   (a) Stone buttresses at each corner provide the building's main support.

   (b) Couples have an obligation to support one another.

   (c) Regina was unable to explain why her sister had acted so strangely.

5. **proscribe**

   (a) My doctor asked me to take 500 milligrams of vitamin C each day.

   (b) His Quaker beliefs did not permit him to take up arms for war.

   (c) Paulina was allowed to leave the grounds whenever she chose.

bereft
criterion
deride
effrontery
espouse
hypocrisy
impending
incensed
pertinent
promulgate
proscribe
redress
regime
retribution
substantiate

6. effrontery

(a) The captain, exhorting his men to follow, charged up the hill.

(b) The driver hit me from behind and then claimed that I'd backed into him.

(c) After pulling the wrong tooth, the dentist wanted to charge me $120.

7. substantiate

(a) The medication is efficacious, and I have the data to prove it.

(b) Enormous heat and pressure at the sun's core convert hydrogen to helium.

(c) The author's footnotes make it unnecessary to accept her claims on faith.

8. regime

(a) France's Bourbon monarchy lasted from 1589 to 1830.

(b) Florence is the capital of Italy's Tuscany region.

(c) From 1933 to 1945, Germany was ruled by the Nazis.

9. derision

(a) I made up my mind that from now on I would choose my friends with care.

(b) The audience roared with laughter when the clown got a pie in the face.

(c) Cries of "Sit down!" and "Boring!" induced Simon to bring his talk to a close.

10. redress

(a) I forwarded Rita's mail to her new home in California.

(b) Davendra demanded that the newspaper's editor apologize for its misstatements.

(c) Those wrongfully imprisoned deserve more than an apology from the state.

18E Passage

Read the passage below; then complete the exercise that follows it.

Prisoners of Conscience

When the United Nations **promulgated** its Universal Declaration of Human Rights in 1948, it was a significant event in world history. No longer would a government be able to say that the treatment of citizens within its borders was an "internal matter" and none of the world's business. This historic document calls for minimum standards of decent treatment for a country's citizens; for example, Article 5 **proscribes** torture, while Article 9 states that no one shall be subject to arbitrary arrest, detention, or exile. Nevertheless, many governments throughout the world pay lip service to such human rights while routinely abusing their citizens. **Hypocrisy** of this kind exists because the United Nations lacks the power to consistently enforce the Declaration's 30 articles.

In 1961, Portugal was ruled by the autocratic Antonio Salazár, who denied the Portuguese people the right to express their political opinions freely. When two students had the **effrontery** to raise their glasses publicly in a toast "to freedom," **retribution** followed swiftly. The two were arrested and sentenced to seven years' imprisonment. A London lawyer named Peter Benenson was **incensed** when he heard of their plight and organized a letter-writing campaign that bombarded the Salazár government with demands for the students' release. Because of the embarrassing publicity his government was receiving, and in order to put the affair behind him, Salazár released the pair.

Benenson's success inspired him to expand his efforts, and he soon found there was no shortage of cases crying out for action. The world's jails were filled with people **bereft** of hope who had committed no crimes but who, for one reason or another, had run afoul of the **regimes** in their countries. The idea that those responsible would heed letters of protest from people outside their borders was **derided** by critics as utterly futile, but Benenson was not deterred. His appeals received an outpouring of support. By the end of 1961 he had formed the human rights advocacy group Amnesty International.

In 1991, Amnesty International (AI) marked its thirtieth anniversary. In 1997, it had more than one million members in 4,300 local groups around the world and was working on behalf of more than 4,000 prisoners of conscience in at least 87 countries. Before "adopting" someone as a prisoner of conscience, AI ensures that the person meets certain **criteria**. Persons detained because of their religious or political views, racial or ethnic origin, or gender, in violation of the Universal Declaration of Human Rights—and who have not **espoused** violence—are eligible for adoption.

AI employs teams of trained investigators to gather information **pertinent** to each case and, if possible, to **substantiate** allegations of abuse—an often difficult task, given that many governments practicing human rights abuses are less than cooperative. In cases where the government involved wishes to avoid public castigation, however, the **impending** arrival of an AI team can sometimes result in the release of prisoners, though the government might not admit the connection between AI and the prisoners' release.

Once adopted, a prisoner of conscience becomes the concern of one or more local chapters to whom the case is assigned. Members send letters and telegrams to the appropriate officials, who may include a country's president, minister of justice, chief judge, or prison warden, asking them firmly and politely to **redress** the wrong that has been done. In a substantial number of cases, this approach has worked; Amnesty International was awarded the 1977 Nobel Peace Prize in recognition of its determined efforts to bring freedom, justice, and peace to the world.

Answer each of the following questions in the form of a sentence. If a question does not contain a vocabulary word from this lesson's word list, use one in your answer. Use each word only once.

1. Give an example of official government **hypocrisy**.

bereft
criterion
deride
effrontery
espouse
hypocrisy
impending
incensed
pertinent
promulgate
proscribe
redress
regime
retribution
substantiate

2. Why did those speaking out in Salazár's Portugal in 1960 face **retribution**?

3. From whose perspective is the reference to the students' "**effrontery**" made?

4. Why was the Universal Declaration of Human Rights **promulgated**?

5. Why is Amnesty International so important to prisoners of conscience?

6. What kind of letters do AI members send?

7. How does AI ensure that it is not misused or manipulated?

8. How does AI choose prisoners of conscience?

9. Why would an **impending** military overthrow of a democratic government concern AI?

10. Why do you think the behavior **proscribed** by the Universal Declaration of Human Rights has not stopped?

 FUN & FASCINATING FACTS

When we **deride** someone, we are, in effect, laughing at that person. The word itself suggests this. It comes from the Latin *ridere*, "to laugh." Three adjectives share this root. *Derisive* means "mocking" or "jeering." (*Derisive* laughter greeted the announcement.) *Risible* means "capable of provoking laughter." (Drake tries to sound intelligent by using long words but only succeeds at being *risible*.) *Derisory* means "worthy of being derided; ridiculous." (I rejected her *derisory* offer of a thousand dollars for my car.)

Regimen (Lesson 3) and **regime** have overlapping meanings in that both can mean government rule or control and both can mean a regular system of diet, exercise, or therapy to promote health. However, it is preferable to keep the two words separate and common usage makes this distinction: a *regimen* is a regular system of diet, exercise, or therapy to promote health; a *regime* is government rule or control.

Lesson 19

Word List
Study the definitions of the words below; then do the exercises for the lesson.

aegis
ē´ jis

n. Protection; sponsorship.
The peacekeeping force entered the area under the **aegis** of the United Nations.

bauble
bô´ bəl

n. A showy, ornamental object with little practical use; a trinket.
When returning from his travels abroad, Father usually brought a colorful **bauble** for each child.

complaisant
kəm plā´ sənt

adj. Willing to please; agreeable.
Jared was **complaisant** toward his boss, carrying out her orders with alacrity and always speaking respectfully to her.

consolidate
kən säl´ i dāt

v. 1. To join together; to unite.
The meeting was convened to discuss **consolidating** the multifarious companies into a single large corporation.
2. To strengthen or make firm.
The candidate's primary victories **consolidated** her position as presidential front-runner.

depredation
dep rə dā´ shən

n. The act of plundering or destroying; also, the loss or damage that results.
Though no lives were lost, the **depredations** inflicted by the hurricane were severe.

epiphany
ē pif´ ə nē

n. A sudden understanding of the meaning, essence, or reality of something.
After many days of agonizing introspection, Gabrielle had an **epiphany** in which the choice to make became unexpectedly clear.

moratorium
môr ə tôr´ ē əm

n. A waiting period or temporary ban on activity.
Hoping to ease the hostility developing between the two countries, the diplomats requested a one-month **moratorium** on troop movements.

pendulous
pen´ jə ləs

adj. Hanging loosely or swinging freely.
The **pendulous** branches of the weeping willow grazed the ground.

portend
pôr tend´

v. To be a sign of; to indicate what will happen.
The high election turnout **portends** a renewed interest in town government.
portent *n.*
The radical new car design may be a **portent** of things to come.
portentous *adj.* (pôr ten´ təs)
There are still those who think that the alignment of the planets is a **portentous** event.

pragmatic
prag mat´ ik

adj. Concerned with practical solutions rather than abstract theory.
Always **pragmatic**, Dorothy was more interested in how she could use the new machine than in the theory behind its design.

reprieve
rē prēv´

v. To delay or suspend punishment.
The condemned man will be executed unless **reprieved** by the governor.
n. A relief or respite, especially when temporary.
Commuters were relieved when the rail line due to be shut down was granted a **reprieve**.

| **stentorian** | *adj.* Extremely loud or powerful in sound. |
| sten tôr´ ē ən | The principal was a charismatic speaker whose **stentorian** voice commanded instant attention. |

| **tenure** | *n.* The condition of holding property, an office, or a position; also the period during which it is held. |
| ten´ yər | The professor's **tenure** at the college ended when she was fired. |

| **unilateral** | *adj.* Done or carried out by one of two or more parties rather than in concert with others. |
| yōōn ə lat´ ər əl | Instead of consulting with other countries, France made a **unilateral** decision to resume nuclear testing in the Pacific. |

viable	*adj.* 1. Capable of living, growing, or developing.
vī´ ə bəl	Less than half of last year's corn seed turned out to be **viable**; the rest did not produce any plants.
	2. Capable of success; workable.
	Although Young-sook's strategy for recycling the city's refuse seemed the most **viable** one, it received only a modicum of support.

19A Understanding Meanings

Read the sentences below. If a sentence correctly uses the word in bold, write *C* on the line below it. If a sentence is incorrect, rewrite it so that the vocabulary word in bold is used correctly.

1. A **bauble** is an object that gives pleasure but lacks usefulness.

_____

2. A **portent** is a sign of what will happen in the future.

_____

3. A **stentorian** voice is one that is melodious.

_____

4. A **pendulous** object is one that sways as it hangs.

_____

5. An **epiphany** is an act of retaliation.

_____

6. To **consolidate** elements is to combine them into a whole.

_____

7. A **reprieve** is a delay in carrying out an action.

8. A **unilateral** move is one made to the side.

9. A **viable** plan is one capable of being carried out successfully.

10. The law's **aegis** is the protection it offers.

11. **Tenure** is living in rented space.

12. A **complaisant** person is one who is self-satisfied.

13. A **moratorium** is a moment set aside to remember those who died.

14. A **pragmatic** person is one who avoids abstract theorizing.

15. **Depredations** are predatory attacks.

aegis
bauble
complaisant
consolidate
depredation
epiphany
moratorium
pendulous
portend
pragmatic
reprieve
stentorian
tenure
unilateral
viable

19B Using Words

If the word (or a form of the word) in bold fits in a sentence in the group below it, write the word in the blank space. If the word does not fit, leave the space empty.

1. **pragmatic**

   (a) The company's _____ approach to business decisions has allowed it to flourish.

   (b) The poor dog's eyesight is so _____ that he can barely see a thing.

   (c) The senator was _____ enough to know when the race was over.

2. **stentorian**

    (a) The _____ blast of the foghorn warned vessels to stay clear.

    (b) Hercules' _____ strength made him a legendary figure in mythology.

    (c) A Roman _____ had command of approximately one hundred men.

3. **pendulous**

    (a) _____ vines hung from the trees, swaying gently in the breeze.

    (b) Zola remained _____ even after others confirmed Carl's fantastic story.

    (c) The old clock's _____ swung gracefully from side to side.

4. **depredation**

    (a) A high fence protects the garden against the _____ of woodchucks.

    (b) The _____ of war had left Atlanta a smoking ruin.

    (c) New drugs offer some protection against the _____ of the AIDS virus.

5. **viable**

    (a) The economic task force came up with a _____ plan to revitalize the city.

    (b) A fetus is considered _____ when it can live outside the mother's womb.

    (c) If you rent a car, you could be held _____ for any damage done to it.

6. **portend**

    (a) A comet in the sky once was believed to _____ misfortune.

    (b) The loss of the potato crop could _____ famine for the region.

    (c) How long the stock market will continue to rise is impossible to _____ .

7. **consolidate**

    (a) I took out a loan to _____ my debts and now make one monthly payment.

    (b) Before the army could _____ its position, the enemy counterattacked.

    (c) The six colleges have agreed to _____ as a single, large university.

8. **complaisant**

    (a) I can borrow anything I need from our _____ neighbors.

    (b) Don't take advantage of your friends just because they are so _____ .

    (c) He was _____ enough to think he could pass the test without studying.

19C Word Study

Change each of the <u>nouns</u> below into an <u>adjective</u> by changing or dropping the suffix or by adding the correct suffix. Write the word in the space provided. Both forms of all of the words in this exercise are from this or an earlier lesson.

<u>Noun</u>	<u>Adjective</u>
1. antithesis	_____
2. metropolis	_____
3. portent	_____
4. parsimony	_____
5. hypocrisy	_____

Change each of the <u>verbs</u> below into a <u>noun</u> by changing or dropping the suffix or by adding the correct suffix. Write the word in the space provided.

<u>Verb</u>	<u>Noun</u>
6. indoctrinate	_____
7. portend	_____
8. oust	_____
9. deride	_____
10. espouse	_____

Change each of the <u>adjectives</u> below into a <u>noun</u> by changing or dropping the suffix or by adding the correct suffix. Write the word in the space provided.

aegis
bauble
complaisant
consolidate
depredation
epiphany
moratorium
pendulous
portend
pragmatic
reprieve
stentorian
tenure
unilateral
viable

<u>Adjective</u>	<u>Noun</u>
11. listless	_____
12. altruistic	_____
13. introspective	_____
14. notorious	_____
15. autocratic	_____

19D Images of Words

Circle the letter of each sentence that suggests the numbered bold vocabulary word. In each group, you may circle more than one letter or none at all.

1. **epiphany**

   (a) Staring at the meat on her plate, Doris realized she was now a vegetarian.

   (b) Seated beneath a tree, the future Buddha suddenly understood the meaning of human suffering.

   (c) Last year Clint followed all the golf tournaments; this year he's only interested in tennis.

2. **pragmatic**

   (a) Ms. Green had no formal philosophy guiding her decisions in life.

   (b) We planned our route carefully to avoid the interstate highways.

   (c) The president's "realpolitik" emphasized practical realism in foreign affairs.

3. **tenure**

   (a) The trust allows Ms. Steinberg to occupy the house during her lifetime.

   (b) Professor Rich cannot be fired simply because the dean dislikes him.

   (c) A United States senator's term of office runs for six years.

4. **portent**

   (a) Scientists are troubled by the depletion of the earth's ozone layer.

   (b) This extremely powerful drug is available only by prescription.

   (c) By a narrow margin, the people of Ireland voted to make divorce legal.

5. **viable**

   (a) Its economy is so strong that Quebec could succeed as an independent nation.

   (b) The baby was born four weeks early, but is perfectly healthy.

   (c) All of the eggs hatched and produced young chicks.

6. **reprieve**

   (a) The song was so well received that she sang it again for the audience.

   (b) The grant means that the theater will not have to close its doors after all.

   (c) The prisoner's death sentence was reduced to one of life imprisonment.

7. **moratorium**

   (a) The service to honor the war dead was held in Washington Cathedral.

   (b) Cod fishing off Georges Bank has been banned for two years.

   (c) Reporters had to wait twenty-four hours before breaking the story.

8. **aegis**

   (a) The American Red Cross's national headquarters is in Washington, D.C.

   (b) The Parents' Association will hold a children's concert this Friday.

   (c) The Horticultural Society sponsors the Boston Flower Show held each March.

9. **bauble**

   (a) Shake the glass ball and snow swirls around a snowman inside it.

   (b) A wealthy buyer paid over $100,000 for the famous gem-crusted egg.

   (c) This useful little gadget is a combination hair dryer and travel iron.

10. **unilateral**

   (a) The U.S. decided to act alone in extending the ban on trade with Cuba.

   (b) When her parents died, Marsha was alone in the world.

   (c) Will other countries join New Zealand in renouncing nuclear weapons?

19E Passage

Read the passage below; then complete the exercise that follows it.

Elephant Memories

Shortly after American journalist Cynthia Moss arrived in Africa as a tourist in 1967, she experienced an **epiphany** that changed her life. Even though it was her first visit to the continent, she later recalled having "this overwhelming sense that I had come home." Africa's growing hold on Moss was **consolidated** when she visited Tanzania and had her first encounter with elephants. Studying these magnificent mammals was to become her life's work.

She returned to Africa the following year and has made her home there ever since. First she worked as a freelance journalist and editor of *Wildlife News*, a publication of the African Wildlife Foundation (AWF). Then, in 1972, under the **aegis** of the AWF, she and another researcher began what would become a long-term study of the elephants of Kenya's Amboseli National Park. They lived among them and carefully noted their behavior. Thanks to Moss's meticulous observations, we now know a great deal about the social life of these complex and highly intelligent creatures.

Elephants travel in extended family groups consisting of immature calves and several generations of cows. These herds are led by the oldest (and often wisest) of the females, the matriarch. Bull calves are driven from the herd when they reach maturity and subsequently travel alone or with two or three other males so that they will find mates from other groups. Moss noted the strong bonds that grow between individuals. In her book *Elephant Memories*, she describes a touching encounter between two herds that met at a waterhole. Individuals greeted each other by gently intertwining their **pendulous** trunks and clicking their tusks together. At the same time, their **stentorian** trumpeting filled the air with conspicuous expressions of joy. Elephants also appear to experience grief over the death of a comrade. Moss has observed herd members trying to "bury" a dead elephant by covering its body with branches and dirt. They maintain vigils, sometimes for many hours, over the corpse of a dead relative.

The beginning of Moss's **tenure** as director of the Amboseli Elephant Research Project coincided with a mounting worldwide demand for ivory carvings that caused the price of this coveted material to increase dramatically over a twenty-year period to about $125 a pound. These carvings were not mere **baubles**, but intricately crafted art objects whose workmanship made them highly tempting to dealers and collectors alike. This rapidly escalating demand

aegis
bauble
complaisant
consolidate
depredation
epiphany
moratorium
pendulous
portend
pragmatic
reprieve
stentorian
tenure
unilateral
viable

portended the extinction of the African elephant, the chief source of ivory, unless drastic action was taken. Marauding bands of poachers armed with powerful automatic weapons rampaged through central and east Africa, slaughtering an average of 2,000 elephants per week during the 1980s simply for their tusks. By bribing **complaisant** government officials to turn a blind eye to their illegal activity, the poachers operated with near impunity. The result was that in the decade prior to 1989, Africa's elephant population declined from 1.3 million to about 600,000.

Cynthia Moss, her longtime associate Joyce Poole, and others concerned about the elephant's plight began a vigorous campaign to save the African elephant. The government of Kenya adopted the **pragmatic** view that live elephants were of more value than the tusks of dead ones since tourists, drawn by East Africa's remarkable wildlife, provided much of the country's income. With the backing of international conservation organizations it began to enforce the laws against poaching, and in 1989, the president of Kenya made headlines throughout the world by lighting a bonfire fueled by over ten tons of ivory confiscated from poachers—a symbolic act intended to dramatize Kenya's **unilateral** ban on ivory trading.

Other African countries followed Kenya's lead, and the following year the Convention on International Trade in Endangered Species, to which over 145 countries belong, declared a **moratorium** on the trading of ivory. The price of ivory plummeted, and poaching suddenly became a less **viable** occupation, though some illegal trading continues. Whether the African elephant has been saved from extinction or merely given a temporary **reprieve** is still an open question. Cynthia Moss is cautiously optimistic. "If the ban stays in place . . . things will improve," she says. But she also points out that it will take several decades before the herds recover from the **depredations** of the 1970s and 1980s. A further complication is that some countries, whose economies depended on the ivory trade to survive, have been allowed to resume limited trade in ivory. Even before this resumption of trade, there were indications that poaching was on the rise despite the ban. It appears to continue to increase today. For many reasons, the future of African elephants remains in doubt.

Answer each of the following questions in the form of a sentence. If a question does not contain a vocabulary word from this lesson's word list, use one in your answer. Use each word only once.

1. What caused the **depredation** of elephant herds at the end of the twentieth century?

_____

2. How might one become aware of the presence of elephants even if they aren't in view?

_____

3. How do elephants show attachment to and fondness for each other?

_____

4. What was Cynthia Moss's **epiphany**?

_____

5. How are the ivory carvings different from **baubles**?

_____

6. What is the structure of an elephant herd?

7. How do you know that Moss is not complacent about the future of African elephants?

8. Why was the Kenyan government unwilling to be **complaisant** toward the ivory poachers?

9. What do you think the return to poaching **portends**?

10. What effect did Kenya's **unilateral** ban on ivory trading have?

FUN & FASCINATING FACTS

According to ancient Greek mythology, Zeus, king of the gods, had been nursed as a baby by a she-goat, an animal that thereafter held special meaning for him. In his victorious battle against the Titans, giants who ruled the earth, Zeus was protected by a shield made from a goatskin, the Greek word for which is *aigis*. Aigis or **aegis** came to mean first a shield, then any form of protection, a meaning it retains in English.

The meanings of *complacent* and **complaisant** should be carefully distinguished. To be *complaisant* is to be agreeable and anxious to please; to be *complacent* is to be self-satisfied and see no need for self-improvement. One can be complaisant without being self-satisfied, and one can be complacent without being agreeable to others. And people who see no room for improvement in themselves and are agreeable *and* eager to please are being simultaneously complacent and complaisant.

The *Iliad* is the title of a long epic poem usually credited to the ancient Greek poet Homer. Composed sometime before 700 B.C., it tells of the war between the Greek and Trojan armies. Our word **stentorian** is derived from a character who appears in the poem. His name was Stentor; he was a herald, whose job was to proclaim messages. For this, he needed a loud, strong voice. Thus, *stentorian* is used to describe such a voice.

Lesson 20

Word List
Study the definitions of the words below; then do the exercises for the lesson.

ambidextrous
am bi deks′ trəs

adj. Able to use both hands with equal skill.
Ambidextrous batters in baseball are called switch hitters.

antipathy
an tip′ ə thē

n. A consistent aversion or dislike.
Despite her **antipathy** to modern art, Deonna is a staunch supporter of the museum.

deleterious
del ə tir′ ē əs

adj. Hurtful; injurious.
A diet high in fats has a **deleterious** effect on one's health.

excoriate
eks kôr′ ē āt

v. To criticize severely; to berate.
Incensed storeowners **excoriated** the mayor for the town's perfunctory snow-clearing efforts.

extrapolate
ek strap′ ə lāt

v. To estimate or infer by projecting from or expanding upon known information.
From a small sample one can **extrapolate** the total number of viewers of a television program.

grisly
griz′ lē

adj. Horrible to contemplate or look upon; grim and ghastly.
Rescue workers had the **grisly** task of looking for bodies following the conflagration that destroyed the rooming house.

idiosyncrasy
id ē ō siŋ′ krə sē

n. A peculiar characteristic, habit, or manner that distinguishes a person.
Wearing a pink cashmere sweater was one of movie director Ed Wood's **idiosyncrasies**.
idiosyncratic *adj.*
Glenn Gould's **idiosyncratic** piano playing was unique and highly personal, and inspired both admiration and animosity from critics.

impute
im py͞oot′

v. To assign blame or credit; to attribute or ascribe.
The children **imputed** to their car a mind and personality of its own.

maladroit
mal ə droit′

adj. Lacking judgment or skill; bungling or clumsy.
Dale's cross-examination of the witnesses was so **maladroit** and ineffective that he was taken off the case.

negate
ni gāt′

v. 1. To deny or refute the existence or truth of.
By pretending all was well I **negated** my true feelings.
2. To make ineffective or invalid.
The surprising results of the new study **negated** previous assumptions about heart disease.

passé
pa sā′

(A French word now part of our vocabulary.) *adj.* No longer in fashion; outmoded.
Nowadays, dressing in formal clothes for dinner is considered **passé** even in the most patrician circles.

pedagogue
ped′ ə gäg

n. A teacher of children or youth; sometimes one who is dogmatic or overly formal.
After teaching all day at school, Mrs. Levendusky also played the **pedagogue** at home, helping her children learn to read.
pedagogical *adj.* (ped ə gä′ jik əl) Of or relating to the science or art of teaching.
Teachers are required by law to regularly update their **pedagogical** skills.

179

preponderance
prē pän´ dər əns

n. The greater part; superiority in size, importance, or strength.
The **preponderance** of cars on the road today are foreign imports; one sees very few domestic models.

propound
prə pound´

v. To put forward for consideration; to propose.
Einstein **propounded** the startling idea that time is elastic and can expand and contract.

stance
stans

n. 1. The way a person stands; the position of a person's feet.
The proper **stance** for this exercise is feet apart with knees slightly bent.
2. A position regarding politics or ideas; point of view.
The candidate modified her **stance** on welfare after studying the issue more closely.

20A Understanding Meanings

Read the sentences below. If a sentence correctly uses the word in bold, write *C* on the line below it. If a sentence is incorrect, rewrite it so that the vocabulary word in bold is used correctly.

1. A **preponderance** of items is the greater number of them.

_____

2. To **extrapolate** a figure is to estimate it from a small sample.

_____

3. A **pedagogical** approach is one that stresses learning by memorizing.

_____

4. To **propound** a theory is to expose it as false.

ambidextrous   _____

antipathy

deleterious

excoriate   5. Someone's **stance** on a subject is that person's point of view.

extrapolate   _____

grisly

idiosyncrasy

impute   6. An **ambidextrous** person is one who has trouble deciding.

maladroit   _____

negate

passé   7. A **grisly** scene is one that provokes horror or disgust.

pedagogue

preponderance   _____

propound

stance

8. To **excoriate** someone is to exalt that person above all others.

9. If something is **passé** it is considered out-of-date.

10. **Antipathy** is a strong feeling of aversion.

11. **Idiosyncrasies** are minor peculiarities of behavior.

12. To **negate** something is to prove it to be true.

13. A **maladroit** person is someone who is adept.

14. To **impute** a fault is to attribute it to someone.

15. A **deleterious** substance is one that has a harmful effect.

20B Using Words

If the word (or a form of the word) in bold fits a sentence in the group below it, write the word in the blank. If the word does not fit, leave the space empty.

1. **deleterious**

   (a) Sandra was _____ with joy when her college of choice sent a letter of acceptance.

   (b) If she knows smoking is _____ to her health, why doesn't she quit?

   (c) The _____ effect of acid rain on lakes has been well documented.

2. **grisly**

(a) Two U.N. peacekeepers made the _____ discovery of several mass graves.

(b) Edgar Allan Poe's _____ tales have enthralled six generations of readers.

(c) That _____ scene where the dead rise from their graves terrified us.

3. **negate**

(a) The two parties were under court order to _____ until they found a compromise.

(b) The Supreme Court will _____ previous rulings if it upholds the appeal.

(c) The new law will _____ the regulation already on the books.

4. **stance**

(a) It was Carl Sagan's _____ that life is widespread in the universe.

(b) The United States eased its _____ regarding trade with China.

(c) Safia's free-throw shooting _____ looks exactly as the coach taught it.

5. **impute**

(a) Scientists _____ that coal reserves in the U.S. should last 300 years.

(b) Don't _____ dishonest traits to Luther on the basis of one brief meeting.

(c) Dee tends to _____ only the finest qualities to a new boyfriend.

6. **propound**

(a) Dave _____ marriage to Christa while they were on vacation.

(b) Dr. Jackson will _____ an alternate theory that comports with the known facts.

(c) Maribel continues to _____ the notion that money should be in the form of gold.

7. **ambidextrous**

(a) We noticed Jessica was _____ when she began drawing as well with her right hand as with her left.

(b) Sparky manages the team in such an _____ manner that he's irreplaceable.

(c) Having one arm in a cast is not a serious problem for an _____ person.

8. **excoriate**

(a) Several members were _____ from the club for dilatory payment of dues.

(b) Mama was an autocrat who _____ her children for the slightest fault.

(c) Eating too much and exercising too little has _____ the patient's heart.

ambidextrous

antipathy

deleterious

excoriate

extrapolate

grisly

idiosyncrasy

impute

maladroit

negate

passé

pedagogue

preponderance

propound

stance

20C Word Study

Complete the analogies by selecting the pair of words whose relationship most resembles the relationship of the pair in capital letters. Circle the letter in front of the pair you choose.

1. CITY : METROPOLITAN ::
   (a) environs : peripheral
   (b) horse : equestrian
   (c) nation : patriotic
   (d) village : rural

2. PRECEPT : INSTRUCT ::
   (a) privation : thrive
   (b) increment : supplement
   (c) revelation : conceal
   (d) buttress : strengthen

3. IMPECUNOUS : WEALTH ::
   (a) listless : energy
   (b) imperturbable : equanimity
   (c) passé : stupidity
   (d) penitent : guilt

4. AUTOCRACY : DEMOCRACY ::
   (a) monarch : kingdom
   (b) one : many
   (c) order : anarchy
   (d) rule : ruler

5. ANNOYED : INCENSED ::
   (a) parsimonious : wealthy
   (b) aristocratic : patrician
   (c) perfunctory : thorough
   (d) hurtful : virulent

6. LOUD : STENTORIAN ::
   (a) original : hackneyed
   (b) famous : notorious
   (c) unfriendly : bellicose
   (d) calm : frenetic

7. MALADROIT : SKILL ::
   (a) crass : sensitivity
   (b) parsimonious : frugality
   (c) craven : fear
   (d) autocratic : confidence

8. NEGATE : AFFIRM ::
   (a) expunge : erase
   (b) oust : ensconce
   (c) scatter : disperse
   (d) impute : impugn

9. PEDAGOGUE : KNOWLEDGE ::
   (a) stoic : concern
   (b) philistine : envy
   (c) raconteur : opprobrium
   (d) athlete : agility

10. BAUBLE : VALUE ::
    (a) platitude : originality
    (b) phobia : fear
    (c) soliloquy : speech
    (d) tundra : expanse

20D Images of Words

Circle the letter of each sentence that suggests the numbered bold vocabulary word. In each group, you may circle more than one letter or none at all.

1. excoriate

(a) Tim gave the teacher the names of the boys who were harassing him.

(b) The government seized the man's property when he refused to pay taxes.

(c) Abby's torn knee ligament caused her intense pain.

2. idiosyncrasy

(a) Ms. Wilkie took care to avoid stepping on cracks in the pavement.

(b) The American poet e. e. cummings chose not to use uppercase letters.

(c) Mr. Dabney was never seen without a fresh flower in his buttonhole.

3. ambidextrous

(a) When Rosario said "him," was she referring to Richardson or González?

(b) One picture was drawn with her left hand and one with her right.

(c) Part of me wants to go with you, and the other wants to stay home.

4. extrapolate

(a) By polling 1,000 people, we can estimate how many city residents expect to vote.

(b) She went on at great length about the advantages of living in the country.

(c) They met three rude Scots and now think that all Scottish people are rude.

5. passé

(a) Car makers no longer make vehicles with huge tail fins and lots of chrome.

(b) The new Z1-Turbo can overtake every other car on the road today.

(c) Genuine fur coats are now seldom worn.

6. pedagogue

(a) Mr. Jacobsen began by making his students memorize the Greek alphabet.

(b) Shirley's doctor gave her shoe inserts to help her flat feet.

(c) That one bad experience taught Anna a lesson she'll never forget.

7. maladroit

(a) Miles rose to shake hands, knocking over the table as he did so.

(b) Continually referring to Sid's wife as his mother did not endear you to her.

(c) The car has a tendency to drift to the right when the brakes are applied.

ambidextrous

antipathy

deleterious

excoriate

extrapolate

grisly

idiosyncrasy

impute

maladroit

negate

passé

pedagogue

preponderance

propound

stance

8. **preponderance**

(a) The sun is made up mostly of hydrogen with small amounts of other gases.

(b) Over sixty percent of voters surveyed declared themselves Independent.

(c) Most of the world's fresh water is locked in the polar ice caps.

9. **deleterious**

(a) Kenji was so ill that he began to hallucinate.

(b) Losing our star quarterback has reduced our chances of winning the game.

(c) We discovered that the house's foundations are riddled with termites.

10. **antipathy**

(a) Lars believed that teaching would be detrimental to his poetry writing.

(b) Toni always says you couldn't get her to take a cruise if you paid her.

(c) Even though these children are twins, they have completely different personalities.

20E Passage

Read the passage below; then complete the exercise that follows it.

It's a Right-Handed World!

Left-handers make up only about 10–15 percent of the population, but they have received more than their share of hostility. A source no less revered then the Bible reflects this longstanding **antipathy**: it contains more than 100 favorable references to the right hand and about 25 unfavorable references to the left hand. Throughout history, all kinds of character flaws have been **imputed** to lefties, and as recently as 1937 Sir Cyril Burt, a well-known British educational psychologist, **excoriated** them in these terms: "They squint, they stammer, they shuffle and shamble, they flounder about like seals out of water."

Burt promulgated the view that left-handedness in children is an **idiosyncrasy** that must be corrected early—a view that was widely accepted among British and American **pedagogues**. One justification was that left-handed children are often **maladroit**; which of course seems to be the case when they are required to use tools, such as scissors, designed exclusively for the right hand. We now know that forcing lefties to use their right hand can have a **deleterious** effect; compelled to do something that does not come naturally, they fare poorly at a variety of tasks and their self-esteem can suffer.

Left-handers were given something else to worry about in 1991 when psychologists Stanley Coren and Diane Halpern **propounded** the theory that they died earlier than right-handed people did. The two studied the death certificates of about one thousand individuals, noting the ages at which the people had died and finding out from family members whether they were right- or left-handed. The average left-hander had died at 66, while the right-handers lived on average to be 75. Other scientists, not all of them lefties, felt that **extrapolating** from such a small sample to the population as a whole was suspect, and expressed the view that a study with far more subjects might **negate** Coren and Halpern's findings. So far, a majority of similar studies has not been able to replicate their results.

The debate that followed once again brought the question of human handedness to the forefront in the psychological community, and raised many questions for which there are as yet no answers. Truly **ambidextrous** persons are rare, and yet our two hands are mirror images of each other, so what causes one to be dominant? And why is there such a **preponderance** of right-handers? Has this always been the case? Most scientists agree that apes and other nonhuman primates do not favor one hand over the other, while human babies exhibit a propensity to do so at about two years old or later. We also suspect that handedness is not genetic because one identical twin may be right-handed and the other left-handed, but this issue is far from being resolved.

The question of whether right-handedness has always been prevalent is a difficult one, but the answer seems to be in the affirmative. Five-thousand-year-old tools such as bronze sickles seem to have been made exclusively for right-handers, while stone tools from earlier periods similarly fit the right hand better than the left. A more **grisly** sort of evidence, hundreds of thousands of years old, points to the same conclusion. Ancient skulls have been found showing injuries caused by frontal blows to the head. These blows occurred far more frequently on the left side, indicating that the assailants were generally right-handed.

The view that left-handedness is a defect in need of correction is thankfully now **passé**; lefties can buy specially designed scissors and tools, though cars and other kinds of heavy equipment are still built only for right-handers. That may explain why, according to Coren and Halpern's study at least, left-handers are five times more likely to die in accidents. Perhaps such discouraging statistics affected the outcome of Coren and Halpern's study; certainly they point to the need for greater understanding and accommodation of left-handedness. One well-documented advantage that lefties have is in the performance of some sports, particularly baseball. A southpaw (another word for a lefty) pitches with the body facing toward first base and can more easily pick off base stealers, while a left-handed batter's **stance** allows for a quicker start when running to first base after hitting the ball. About 30 percent of major-league pitchers are left-handed. And the list of prominent lefties, from Leonardo da Vinci and Ludwig van Beethoven to Bill Gates and Ruth Bader Ginsburg, clearly shows that even in a right-handed world, left-handers thrive.

Answer each of the following questions in the form of a sentence. If a question does not contain a vocabulary word from this lesson's word list, use one in your answer. Use each word only once.

1. What does the evidence tell us about how far back right-handedness goes?

2. Why is evidence from the Stone Age about left- and right-handedness described as **grisly**?

3. Why do we not need to count them all to know that the number of left-handers in the United States averages about 35 million?

4. How has **pedagogical** theory regarding "lefties" changed since the 1930s?

5. How would right-handers perform if forced to use left-handed scissors?

ambidextrous
antipathy
deleterious
excoriate
extrapolate
grisly
idiosyncrasy
impute
maladroit
negate
passé
pedagogue
preponderance
propound
stance

6. In what ways could negative theories **propounded** about left-handedness be harmful, even if they are inaccurate?

7. What advantage is **imputed** to left-handed pitchers in baseball?

8. How does the handedness of apes and other nonhuman primates differ from most humans?

9. How does the passage make clear that the **idiosyncrasy** of left-handedness does not prevent people from succeeding?

10. Why do you think left-handed people have aroused such **antipathy** through the centuries?

FUN & FASCINATING FACTS

The Latin prefix *ambi-* means "both" and appears in several English words. An *ambiguous* statement is one that can be taken two ways. *Ambivalence* is the inability to decide which of two possible courses to follow. This prefix also combines with the Latin *dexter*, "right," to form **ambidextrous**. It is an example of the prejudice against left-handedness since it assumes that it is an ambidextrous person's left hand that measures up to the facility of the right. One could just as well call a person equally skillful with both hands *ambisinstrous*, from the Latin *sinister*, "left," thus suggesting that it is the right hand that is as skillful as the left. This latter root is still another example of the historical bias against, or in this case fear of, left-handedness. A *sinister* person by today's definition is one who is bad, wicked, or evil.

Malaise (Lesson 13) and *malodorous* (Lesson 16) are both formed from the Latin *malus*, "bad." It is combined with *adroit*, "skillful," to form **maladroit**. *Adroit* comes from the French phrase *a droit*, "to the right," another example of the bias in favor of right-handedness embedded in the language.

Review for Lessons 17–20

Crossword Puzzle Solve the crossword puzzle below by studying the clues and filling in the answer boxes. Clues followed by a number are definitions of words in Lessons 17 through 20. The number gives the word list in which the answer to the clue appears.

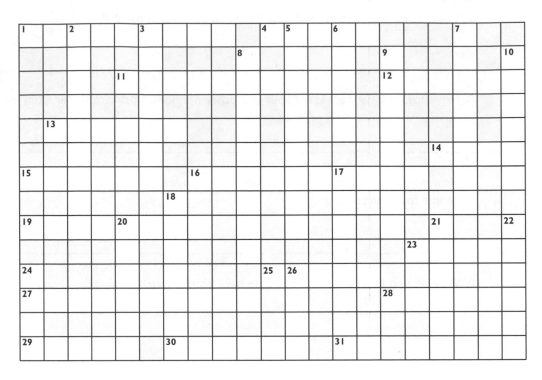

Clues Across

1. Deliberate deception (17)
4. No longer in fashion (20)
11. Exercising sole or complete control (17)
12. A form of rule or government (18)
13. To assign blame or credit (20)
14. Opposite of *easy*
15. Measurement system using grams
16. A temporary ban on an activity (19)
19. Filled with rage (18)
23. Military rank above captain
25. Protection, defense, or sponsorship (19)
27. Carried out by one side only (19)
28. Oranges and lemons are _____ fruits
29. Opposite of *here*
30. The way a person stands (20)
31. A representative sent on a mission (17)

Clues Down

2. Concerned with practical solutions (19)
3. Very sarcastic; sharp or biting (17)
5. A strong feeling of dislike (20)
6. Shoes and _____
7. A sudden understanding or realization (19)
8. To forbid as harmful (18)
9. To put forward for consideration (20)
10. To laugh at in scorn or contempt (18)
17. To delay or suspend punishment (19)
18. To correct or compensate for a wrong (18)
20. To make ineffective or invalid (20)
21. Prickly plant
22. Horrible to contemplate or look upon (20)
24. To eject from a position or place (17)
26. One of the Great Lakes